MONEY AND EXCHANGE DEALING IN INTERNATIONAL BANKING

INTERNATIONAL BANKING SERIES

General Editor: Steven I. Davis

Money and Exchange Dealing in International Banking

Nigel R. L. Hudson

A HALSTED PRESS BOOK

John Wiley & Sons
New York

First published 1979 by
THE MACMILLAN PRESS LTD
London and Basingstoke
Published in the U.S.A
by Halsted Press, a Division
of John Wiley & Sons, Inc.
New York.

Library of Congress Cataloging in Publication Data

Hudson, Nigel R L
  Money and exchange dealing in international banking.

  (International banking series)
  "A Halsted Press book."
  Bibliography: p.
  Includes index.
  1. Foreign exchange administration. 2. Banks and
banking, International. I. Title. II. Series.
HG3851.H8   658'.91'33215   79–15362
ISBN 0–470–26794–1

Printed in Great Britain

Contents

Editor's Foreword

The internationalisation of banking in the 1970s has been one of the most intriguing trends in the financial industry since the Second World War. Whether one measures it by the volume of overseas lending, the modification of traditional banking tenets or changes in physical structures, it is a truly revolutionary development—comparable, for example, to the appearance of international merchant banking in the Renaissance period and the nineteenth-century growth of commercial banks financing trade with the developing countries of the time.

This phenomenon has not, however, been matched by a comparable development in banking literature. While a variety of books have described the theory and structures of the new Euro-markets and the function of the traditional foreign exchange markets, relatively few books have been written about how bankers actually manage their new international responsibilities. Even more exceptional are volumes written by experienced, practising bankers about how they deal with the problems and issues they face.

The purpose of the *International Banking Series* is to fill at least a portion of this gap. While not specifically designed as a series of textbooks, in that it is oriented towards the management issues of international banking, the series does explain how the basic international banking functions are performed, both in theory and in practice. It will hopefully, therefore, serve as a useful reference point for students of banking, individuals who are entering the field of international banking, and outside observers such as customers and academics who would like to know more about how bankers run their international business.

The money-dealing function has justifiably attracted the attention both of outside observers and bankers themselves because of such factors as the vast sums which have been earned—and lost—in deposit and foreign exchange trading in recent years, the vital importance to international banks of funding in the wholesale money markets, and the highly specialist nature of the dealing function, which is accompanied by a unique jargon and set of operating practices.

Mr Hudson's book, therefore, aims at dissipating some of the mystery which has surrounded this vital function by explaining for the uninitiated how, both in theory and practice, a dealer performs his essential tasks of bidding for deposits, running a deposit mismatch book, meeting customer requirements for foreign exchange, and operating a spot and forward foreign exchange book for the bank's own account. A unique contribution is represented by the analysis of the interaction of swap differentials and interest rates, as well as of other dynamic relationships which influence the profitability and liquidity of the dealer's positions. A particular focus is placed on the problems of controlling these critical activities from a management standpoint, evaluating the profit performance of the dealing function, and analysing the issues which are faced by management in operating a world-wide position in foreign exchange and Eurocurrency deposits.

Nigel Hudson's experience in international banking gives him unusually appropriate qualifications for writing this particular volume. An Englishman who has as a dealer experience of the London, Swiss and American markets, in 1970 he joined the London branch of the First National Bank in Dallas, one of the most successful of the American regional banks. During his subsequent career with that bank, he not only moved up the ranks to become chief dealer in London, but also was posted to Paris, where as General Manager he established the bank's Paris branch in 1974, and then returned to London where he took over responsibility for the London branch as Senior Vice-President and General Manager. Such a relatively unusual career, therefore, gives him a particularly interesting perspective on the international markets not only as a practising dealer, but also as a senior manager responsible for the dealing function in major operating units.

As general editor of the series, I am particularly indebted to Nigel Hudson for his effort and commitment as reflected in this book. Another volume in the series, *The Management Function in International Banking*, deals with some of the dealing-related issues as perceived by senior management.

London 1978   STEVEN I. DAVIS

Preface

In recent years there has been a rapid growth in money dealing as a result of the increase in international trade, the development of the multinational company, the volatility of the foreign exchange markets and the large and changing surpluses and deficits of countries. This has led to the writing of many books concerned with trade finance, foreign exchange operations and the development of the Euro-currency market.

The purpose of this book is to fill a gap which is believed to exist in the literature concerned with international money dealing. It is intended to be read by those who may wish to become involved with international money dealing but who have not yet acquired the specific skills, as well as by those who are already involved and who wish to obtain another opinion. It has also been written in an attempt to remove some of the mystique which surrounds the subject.

It should be remembered that no two banks or customers react in exactly the same way or have necessarily the same interests. The book also concerns itself with the dealing practices and money markets of major countries and currencies. Consequently, it may be that, in the process of trying to explain and simplify, certain very specialised practices have been excluded.

Within the book there are examples to illustrate particular points. It should be recognised that the rates used may not be the actual rates of exchange or interest rates of a particular day since they are merely examples to assist in the understanding of the subject. Throughout the book, 'US$' means the currency of the United States of America. When the term 'billion' is used, it is to be understood in the United States sense, i.e. to express one thousand million.

All the views and ideas expressed in this book are those of the author and are not necessarily representative of those of the First National Bank in Dallas.

September 1978   NIGEL HUDSON

List of Abbreviations

EEC	European Economic Community
FDIC	Federal Deposit Insurance Corporation
LIBOR	London Interbank Offered Rate
p.a.	per annum
d	discount
p	premium
DM	Deutschmarks
DFls	Dutch guilders
FFcs	French francs
SFcs (SF)	Swiss francs
$	Dollar
US$	US dollars
£	Pound sterling
$/DM	Rate of Exchange US dollars/Deutschmarks
$/SFcs	Rate of Exchange US dollars/Swiss francs
Stg.	Pound Sterling

1 History

Before describing many of the techniques and practices of the foreign exchange and money markets, it might perhaps be useful to provide some basic definitions and examine something of their recent history.

Foreign Exchange	The conversion of one national currency into another.
Money Market(s)	The borrowing or depositing of funds in a given centre or centres.
Eurocurrency	Currency owned by a non-resident of the country of the currency which has been placed on deposit in a market outside the country of the currency.
Eurodollars	US dollars which are owned by non-residents of the USA and which have been placed on deposit in a European money market. (Asian dollars are dollars as above but on deposit in an Asian money market.)

A much longer and more comprehensive glossary will be found on p. 124. Jargon is one of the major difficulties which will be encountered when attempting to understand the foreign exchange and money markets.

INTRODUCTION

People have been exchanging money, lending it and borrowing it for hundreds of years. However, it is only in the last hundred years that trading in its present form has taken place, since it is necessary to have effective communications to transact the

1

dealings of today. As communications have improved, the money markets have improved with them so that today there is a twenty-four-hour foreign exchange and money market on a world-wide basis.

At the beginning of the twentieth century, countries like Great Britain and the United States had implemented the Gold Specie Standard, which meant among other things that

(a) Gold must be legal tender.
(b) All other means of payment must be capable of being exchanged against gold at the central bank.
(c) There must be no restriction of the import or export of gold.

With the expansion of trade and the expanded economies after the First World War, and despite repeated attempts during the period up to 1931, the United Kingdom was obliged to give up the Gold Standard. The period 1918–39 was marked by a number of devaluations (Belgium, France, Holland, Switzerland) and changes to the Gold Specie Standard. During this period, the term 'hard currency' came to be understood. It means a currency which, instead of being convertible into gold, is supported by reserves of currencies which are themselves capable of being converted into gold. During the same period, restrictions on foreign exchange were introduced—the beginnings of exchange control.

Whilst the rest of the book is concerned with the foreign exchange and money market practices of today, it is none the less important to realise what occurred at and before Bretton Woods in 1944 and to understand what it meant when, on 15 August 1971, the USA announced that its currency was no longer convertible into gold. Therefore, the rest of this chapter is concerned with the history of the markets, since dealers must have an appreciation for the history of the money system in which they operate.

BRETTON WOODS

Prior to the end of the Second World War, it was realised that it would be necessary to establish some new international monetary arrangements in order to:

(a) Determine the nature of the asset against which currencies could be valued.
(b) Determine how the payment of imbalances between countries will take place.
(c) See if the 'world's monetary system can be centrally managed rather than being the consequence of individual national decisions'.

Therefore, at Bretton Woods it was agreed that the International Monetary Fund should be established and that all member countries would agree to their currencies being expressed either as being worth a given amount of gold or as being worth a given number of United States dollars. In addition, each member country agreed to see that these values were maintained within a given range. It was further agreed that no deviation from these ranges could occur without the agreement of the International Monetary Fund (IMF). The IMF could not object unless the change exceeded 10 per cent.

At the same time, the United States agreed with the IMF that its currency would always be convertible into gold and that it would in turn always buy and sell gold at a fixed price of $35 per ounce. This became the basis of the US dollar reserve function and also became known as the Gold Exchange Standard.

Gold was, as is generally recognised, the weakness of Bretton Woods. In 1945, the gold stock of the United States was about $20 billion, which was about 60 per cent of the total of official gold reserves. Therefore, at the time this was considered to be sufficient. Even in the late 1950s, the United States' gold reserves exceeded, by a ratio of three to one, the total dollar reserves of all foreign central banks.

What was unforeseen at Bretton Woods was the growth which would take place in US dollar reserves such that between 1951 and 1971 they would increase to the point where they exceeded the gold reserves. As the dollar reserves held by foreign central banks increased, it became essential that their confidence in the USA was maintained since otherwise they would demand conversion into gold at the 1934 price of gold of $35 per ounce.

FROM BRETTON WOODS TO 1967

Whilst there had been dealings in foreign exchange both during and immediately after the Second World War in a number of centres, it was not until the early 1950s, and in the case of London, 1952, that the inter-bank markets were reopened and dealing departments re-established. However, 'free trading' was not permitted, since transactions were governed by Exchange Control Regulations and prices or rates of exchange had been predetermined by Bretton Woods.

In May 1953, authorised banks of eight members of the European Payments Union began cash (spot) transactions and this was soon followed by permission to recommence forward trading. The period of the 1950s was, compared with today, a period of calm. Markets began to become established, improved systems of settling country debts emerged and the European Monetary Agreement of 1958 came into being.

Prior to this, in March 1954, the London Gold Market was reopened. This meant that the freshly-mined gold of South Africa and Russia could be sold in an orderly manner. At this time, about 50 per cent of the total turnover in the markets was believed to have come from central banks. Notwithstanding this, the price of gold hardly moved because of the commitment of the United States to support the US dollar with a price of $35 an ounce. Because of the calm, the tight exchange control regulations and the limited opportunities which were available, banks and their dealers did little more than execute customers' transactions. Therefore, the dealing function in a bank was of little real interest. This was not to last in the 1960s.

In 1960, doubt began to emerge as to whether there was sufficient gold to back the dollar and support world liquidity. This resulted in there being definite pressure on the price of the gold. At the same time, the United States was beginning a recession, incurring an outflow of funds due to interest rate differences between the USA and Europe and spending more in the form of military spending and the provision of aid. There was also about to be a new political administration in the USA with Kennedy succeeding Eisenhower.

The United Kingdom was also beset with problems. Reserves were still low after the war and were lowered even more when in March 1961 money left London for Germany as the German mark had been revalued and there was a view that others might follow. The Dutch did so since both they and Germany had strong balance of payments positions. Switzerland also benefited, about $300 million moving in hectic market conditions in four days. However, the Swiss National Bank then promptly turned round and lent this amount back to the Bank of England to provide the UK with added financial support.

In October 1964, the Labour Party took office and inherited many of the problems of the outgoing government but with one extra disadvantage—lack of confidence in Labour policies from holders of sterling. To counteract this, the Prime Minister, Harold Wilson, made the historic statement in October that he would defend the sterling parity at $2.80. However, such was the pressure that interest rates in London rose, reserves fell and much of the $1 billion of short-term credit facilities were used and it soon became apparent that devaluation was inevitable unless some extra support was provided. Thus, in November 1964, a $3 billion support package was arranged with funds from Germany, Canada, USA, Japan, France, Italy, Switzerland, Sweden, Holland, Austria and the Bank for International Settlements. This support steadied the market for a short while.

At the beginning of 1965, however, confidence again began to wane, so a new incentive by the central banks was attempted—a bear squeeze. In September, the central banks bought sterling, the foreign exchange market was caught unprepared and the Bank of England was able to see its reserves increase again. Thus it reduced some of its debt to the other central banks.

By 1967 (18 November), it was finally recognised that sterling was overvalued and that the economy could not support the rate; and so a devaluation of 14.3 per cent was arranged whereby the parity rate was reduced from $2.80 to $2.40.

1967–1971

If much of the attention of the 1960s had been focused on sterling, it was to be the US dollar, the French franc and the German mark in the period 1967–71.

As a matter of prudence, France had traditionally bought gold for its reserves and tried to lessen its holding of US dollars. In the period 1962–6, it had bought $3 billion from the USA. This had often resulted in gold speculation and foreign exchange speculation. However, in May 1968 rioting broke out in Paris, a general strike was organised, and as foreigners sold French francs the reserves declined. Thus it was necessary for France to sell one third of the gold it had acquired in 1962–6 to enable it to have US dollars with which to support the currency. This was not enough and, as with the pound in 1967, in August 1969 France devalued the French franc by 11.1 per cent. The cost to the reserves was over $5 billion and again it had been demonstrated that even with large central bank credits it was difficult, if not impossible, to stop the inevitable devaluation.

Germany, as well as the United States, had been a recipient of much of the money which had flowed out of the United Kingdom and France. As a consequence, the Deutschmark was revalued in 1969 by 9.3 per cent after a period when it was allowed to float against the US dollar. This meant that Germany was permitting free market forces to help determine the correct value of the currency and not the fixed rates of Bretton Woods. Therefore, it was in many ways the appetiser for what was to happen in 1971.

Whilst the changes in the German and French parities were important, it is the US dollar which began to receive attention.

As has been mentioned, the US dollar was, and is, the cornerstone of the world's reserves. Therefore, whatever happens, the USA is bound to have some effect on other currencies around the world.

At the beginning of the 1960s, the USA had experienced a strong growth in its trade surplus and an increase in capital outflows. Interest rates in the USA were lower than many others, large amounts of credit were available and United States corporations were expanding overseas. Later the United States faced larger and larger expenditures as a result of the Vietnam War. Thus, by 1970, USA gold reserves were down to $11 billion—a fall of 63 per cent in 10 years—and foreign claims on the USA were in excess of $22 billion. This was an unhealthy situation—what would happen if confidence disappeared and foreigners asked for gold instead of dollars? Whilst in 1968 a two-tier gold market had been established with one rate for official settlements between central banks and another rate—a free market rate—for commercial users, it was felt that this too was threatened.

President Nixon had introduced a highly expansionary fiscal policy with a budget deficit of $23 billion in 1971. There was no incomes policy in the USA and so, unless there was a change in the rate of exchange, United States goods would no longer be competitive in world trade. All of this had been recognised but no action had been taken. Thus, early in 1971 dealers began to sense that soon there would be a crisis for the US dollar. Accordingly, corporations, banks and their customers began to be concerned. Billions of US dollars were sold for either immediate or future delivery as a precaution against a change in parity for the US dollar. This was further aggravated by leading and lagging from exporters and importers.

Since German interest rates were relatively high because of a very restrictive domestic credit policy, much of the speculation against the US dollar was in favour of the Deutschmark. Between 3 May and 5 May 1971, over \$2 billion flowed into Germany. This resulted in the Germans allowing their currency to float freely. The guilder also floated. Switzerland and Austria revalued against the US dollar by 7.07 per cent and 5.05 per cent respectively. Japan was also affected and tried to take steps to halt the inflow of funds. Japanese reserves rose over \$2 billion between April and July 1971. Pre-payments on yen borrowings against ships being constructed dominated this move.

Thus, all over the world, dealers felt something had to happen and yet still the United States Government did not react until August, when billions of US dollars left the country. On 15 August 1971, President Nixon announced the closure of the gold window—in other words, the US dollar would no longer be convertible into gold. Immediately, official parities and intervention points were suspended and most major currencies began a clean or a managed float. A clean float is a free float and a managed float is when a central bank intervenes to steady an exchange rate because of a temporary problem. To avoid complete chaos, the markets were closed in many centres for several days after the Nixon announcement to see if some joint policy could be proposed. This failed and so markets reopened and rates moved wildly. Banks and customers tried to protect themselves by hedging. Since much of the business was one way—selling US dollars—the stronger currencies (the Deutschmark and the yen) appreciated.

In an attempt to return to fixed parities, a meeting of the Group of Ten Countries in December 1971 at the Smithsonian Institute in Washington resolved to fix new parities, allow fluctuations of $2\frac{1}{4}$ per cent either side and raise the official price of gold to \$38 per ounce. This was equivalent to a 7.9 per cent devaluation of the US dollar.

Since the parities which were established are now (1978) used as reference points, they are listed below:

Smithsonian Parities against the US dollar

Austria	23.30
Belgium	44.8159
Denmark	6.9800
France	5.1157
Holland	3.2447
Italy	581.50
Japan	308.00
Norway	6.6454
Portugal	27.25
Spain	64.4737
Sweden	4.8129
Switzerland	3.84
United Kingdom	2.6057
West Germany	3.225

Thus, the yen appreciated by 16.88 per cent against the US dollar, the Deutschmark by 13.58 per cent, the French franc by 8.57 per cent and even the pound appreciated by the similar amount of 8.57 per cent. Some monies flowed back to the United States and the year ended on a note of optimism.

1971–1978

The European Economic Community (EEC) in April 1972 undertook to try to limit the fluctuations of their currencies to each other—the first 'snake'.

The feeling that all was well disappeared in mid-1972 as sterling again came under pressure and in June floated free at a further cost to the United Kingdom reserves. Germany (the *bardepot* scheme), Holland, Japan and Switzerland all tried to stop the inflow of funds as dealers again became concerned that further realignment was necessary.

In February 1973, the US dollar was devalued by a further 10 per cent and the official price of gold raised to $42.22 per ounce. This had resulted from the poor trade figures for December which had been announced in January together with the increased buying of Swiss francs after the Italian crisis, also in January.

Pressure continued on the US dollar since by now confidence was low, inflation in the USA was rising and the price of gold was increasing. Notwithstanding a short period of recovery in mid-1973, the future level of the US dollar was still in doubt. However, in late 1973 the Yom Kippur War and the sudden substantial increase in the price of oil caused further turmoil in the markets. Countries without oil would, it was felt, begin to run large deficits just to pay for oil imports. As a result, the US dollar increased in value and the Swiss franc and German mark declined. In 1974 the United States Government removed capital controls (OFDI and VFCR programmes) and so United States banks began lending US dollars to assist them in paying for their oil. Thus immediately the US dollar weakened again as US dollars left the United States.

The rise in the oil price fuelled inflation and led to the beginnings of the recession. At the same time, whilst many countries took steps to increase the price of oil and so cut domestic consumption, the United States did not allow the price of its oil to reach world levels. Accordingly, consumption continued at a high level and the United States became an importer of oil, thereby causing more US dollars to come into foreign hands. Therefore, since 1974 currencies have moved wildly against each other and whilst some European countries have tried to keep their currencies in line with each other if not with the US dollar, it has not been an easy period.

During 1976 there was large-scale intervention in the exchange markets by the central banks because of substantial movements in exchange rates. The most dramatic movements occurred with the weakening of the pound sterling and the Italian lira, and the appreciation of the Deutschmark and Swiss franc. As a result of this unrest, the French franc left the EEC 'snake' in March and the Deutschmark was revalued against other snake currencies in October. Despite the continuing deterioration of the United States Balance of Payments, the US dollar was relatively stable.

Perhaps the most dramatic change in an exchange rate was the decline of the pound sterling caused by the large current account deficit, leading and lagging and the withdrawal of sterling by non-residents. This led to the exchange rate declining to £1 = \$1.55½ in October 1976. The United Kingdom was obliged to negotiate a

$5.3 billion six-month credit facility from other central banks to apply for a stand-by loan of $3.9 billion from the IMF and to increase interest rates to over 15 per cent per annum. Following the intervention of the IMF together with the decline in the value of the US dollar, sounder economic policies from the British Government and the exploitation of North Sea oil, the pound improved in 1977 and 1978, although its value against the US dollar has not appreciated to the same extent as many other currencies.

Since June 1977 it has been the depreciation of the US dollar and the appreciation of other currencies, notably the yen, Swiss franc and Deutschmark, which has dominated the exchange markets. The cause of the decline in value of the US dollar has been the increasing deficit on the current account of the United States balance of payments and the increase in the rate of inflation. Consequently, the United States arranged new and increased swap lines of credit with the German Central Bank to enable it to intervene in the markets. This was unusual in that the United States is normally in favour of an unmanaged exchange rate and feels that markets should be left to find their own levels.

The foreign exchange markets are volatile and with the advent of floating rates the markets have seen large fluctuations in the rates of exchange. As a consequence, the money-lending function in banks has increased in importance to cope with the increased activity required by customers and the need to protect the banks' own exposure.

THE EUROCURRENCY DEPOSIT MARKET

As the various crises occurred in the exchange markets, they had an effect on the deposit markets. It is generally agreed that Eurocurrency deposit trading began when Eastern Bloc countries found themselves with dollar reserves around 1944. Because of the Cold War which occurred soon after the end of the Second World War, the Eastern Bloc nations were concerned that if they placed these funds on deposit in the United States they might be expropriated. To overcome this problem, deposits were placed by Eastern Bloc banks with British banks who in turn reinvested the money in the United States, either by buying Treasury Bills or by placing the funds on deposit with an American bank. In the 1950s and early 1960s, it was realised that these deposits could be used in a more profitable way to finance trade and capital projects.

After the East Europeans, the deposit market was helped in its growth by the introduction of convertibility of foreign exchange, which has already been mentioned. Banks and the newly emerging multinational corporations now had foreign currency balances which they could invest for short periods. The United States' deficits from 1958 also assisted in placing more US dollars in foreign ownership.

In 1964, the United States introduced the Interest Equalisation Tax as a measure to protect their balance of payments. Immediately, United States corporations had to finance their overseas investments offshore and these surplus dollar holdings looked to be an ideal solution.

During the credit squeezes of 1966 and 1969, United States bank branches borrowed Eurocurrency deposits for use by their head offices. They could obtain these funds, as they were not limited in the interest rate which they could pay to the lender. Had they wished to take the same funds in the United States, they would have been precluded by Regulation Q from paying more than a maximum interest rate for a given deposit. Thus, the Eurocurrency deposit market has grown in size to approximately $670 billion dollars with about three-quarters of the deposits held in US dollars.

Eurosterling, Deutschmark, French franc and Swiss franc markets have all been created because foreign nationals have acquired them or governments have tried to control their flow; and hence another parallel market has developed.

As a result of so much turbulence in the foreign exchanges and the creation of this vast pool of Eurocurrency, it is not perhaps surprising that banks as dealers in money should suddenly discover that the international dealing function has an important role to play in their affairs. The remainder of this book is concerned with the techniques used, the problems of control and the resultant profitability.

2 The Dealing Theory of Foreign Exchange

A dealer in money does not need to be an economist to understand what causes an economic change. However, he must appreciate the signals from the economy of a particular country in order to be able to anticipate what this may mean to the rate of exchange. A rate of exchange is defined as the price of one currency in terms of another. It is quoted either for spot settlement (immediate or within two days) or for future or forward delivery.

With the exception of the pound sterling, it is normal to quote the number of units of a particular currency which equal one US dollar. Because of the importance of the pound in the nineteenth century and its being a relatively large purchasing unit, it is the exception, and all currencies tend to be quoted as so many units equal to one pound. In the United States, it is more normal for rates to be quoted as one foreign unit equalling so many dollars or cents.

EXAMPLE 2.1 Spot exchange rates

        Europe: US$1 = 2.1079 Deutschmarks   A
or USA: US$0.4744 = 1 Deutschmark   B
        To calculate: B is the reciprocal of A

$$\therefore \ \frac{1}{2.1079} = 0.4744$$

        But always: £1 = US$1.8954
           or: £1 = 4.0500 Deutschmarks

Having shown how a rate is both defined and quoted, it is now essential to understand upon what basis it was originally calculated.

There are two starting-points for the calculation of a currency:

1. *Mint Par Exchange*: 'Where two countries use the same metal as the basis of their currencies, the Mint Par of Exchange between them is the number of units of the one currency which should legally contain the same amount of pure metal as does legally a given number of units of the other currency.'

Since so few countries now express their currency as being worth so many ounces or grains of fine gold and since it takes no account of the practicability of physical shipment, this is purely a theoretical means of establishing a relationship between the currencies of two nations.

2. *Purchasing Power Parity* 'between any two countries is that amount of the currency of one country which endows the holder with the same amount of purchasing power, i.e. command over goods and services, as would a stated amount of the currency of the other country.'

This theory was expounded by Dr Gustav Cassel of Stockholm after the 1914–18 war. What is meant by this is:

In Country A it takes 5 units of the local currency to buy 1 widget. In Country B it takes 15 units of the local currency to buy 1 widget. ∴ If the rate of exchange between Countries A and B is 1:3, then the widget will cost the same in both countries. The rate of exchange is then at the Purchasing Power Parity. If this parity moves, e.g. the ratio changes to 1:2, then it would become cheaper to purchase in one country as opposed to another. Perhaps this is best shown by Example 2.1.

EXAMPLE 2.2

| *USA* | *Germany* |

$5 buys 1 kilo of widgets   DM15 buys 1 kilo of widgets
        Rate of exchange: $1 = DM3
                ∴ $5 = DM15 (5 ×3)
                ∴ PARITY

        if rate of exchange: $1 = DM2
                then: $5 = *only* DM10 (5 ×2)
Therefore, to obtain DM15, it is necessary to have not $5 but

$7.50. Germany is said to be more expensive and Germans would go to the USA to buy their widgets. This would increase demand for USA widgets, lessen demand for German widgets and thereby cause Germans to buy US dollars and to sell Deutschmarks. According to the Purchasing Power Parity theory, this would continue until the prices of the widgets in the USA equalled the prices in Germany and *parity* was achieved.

WHY RATES OF EXCHANGE MOVE

In reality, trade between two countries is not confined to one article nor to trade in a single direction. However, Example 2.2 is important since when considering a country's balance of trade it is the sum of such examples.

As long as currencies are artificially restricted to a fixed parity, movements in a particular rate of exchange are restricted to a previously agreed band around the central parity rate. With a floating exchange rate, the price is free to move over a much greater range and it is, therefore, sensitive to a variety of factors which can be examined by considering the construction of a country's balance of payments accounts:

Balance of payments account

Exports of merchandise	+ (money received)
Imports of merchandise	− (money paid away)
Trade balance =	**A** (sum)
Exports of services	+ (money received for services rendered)
Imports of services	− (money paid away for services rendered)
Service balance =	**B**
A + **B** =	Current balance
Long-term investment inflow	+
Long-term investment outflow	−
Private and official borrowings	+
Private and official loans	−
Capital balance =	**C**

Current balance + capital
balance = Overall balance
Overall balance if plus = Increase in country's reserves
Overall balance if minus = Decrease in country's
reserves

Significant movements in the above figures will, therefore, lead to a change in a country's rate of exchange since, for example, if the trade balance is minus, the service balance is minus and the capital balance is minus, the country's reserves must ultimately be decreased to zero. At this point, the country is bankrupt. During this time, any foreign holders of the currency would be trying to sell it before it decreased in value and to buy another more attractive currency or commodity. Thus, with more sellers than buyers, the price of the currency and the exchange rate must fall until such time as sellers equal buyers.

This very simple explanation is intended to show just how important it is for the above statistics of a country to be regularly examined. It should always be borne in mind that it is necessary to observe the statistics over a period of time to see if a trend is developing, since often one set of statistics by themselves can be misleading. This is extremely important when considering the trade balance.

The trade balance can be very easily affected by the time-lag of goods moving through Customs, by the import of a very large and expensive piece of equipment in a particular period, or by stockpiling ahead of a change in regulations or price. Some countries always have a minus trade balance but offset this by selling services such as insurance, tourism and transportation. However, if, for example, a country which depends heavily on tourism for increasing its foreign exchange reserves is involved in an internal war, then tourists would not wish to be exposed to the danger and money would cease to flow. Bad weather might also deter them and, suddenly, a country which is already minus on the trade balance would be minus on the current balance in a particular period. Provided this was only temporary, the next set of statistics would show an improvement and the trend line would be back to normal.

Countries lend money to each other officially and unofficially when the transaction is between a resident and a non-resident. A rich country with large reserves may make a loan to a poor country with small reserves. The wealthy country will create a foreign exchange asset and the poor country a liability. To the lending nation will be paid interest, therefore increasing its reserves whilst depleting the reserves of the borrower. The importance of this on spot rate of exchange is that the payment of debts and interest creates a need for foreign exchange and, if a country has high borrowing, it often has a weak currency since it must continually deplete its reserves to repay its debts, and a lender often requires payment in his own currency, *not* that of the borrower.

Large government spending overseas, whilst healthy for a nation with large reserves, is unhealthy for one with small reserves since it could so easily become bankrupt if there was a problem, for example, with its balance of trade. Government spending has always affected the exchanges since many have gone overseas to buy arms since the fifteenth century. Therefore, a government is expected at all times to keep such spending in order and to ensure that it always has a fund available for future contingencies.

A spot foreign exchange rate is also affected or determined by speculation. However, speculation is often confused with anticipation. For example, if the price of a currency is expected to rise, an exporter will delay demanding payment for as long as possible so that when he receives the foreign currency he will, upon conversion, receive more of the local currency than before. An importer, on the other hand, will either buy as much as he can for stock whilst the price is right or try to pay immediately. This is called 'leading and lagging', which is occurring at all times. It is almost impossible to be precise about the effect of leading and lagging on the exchange market since it is difficult to monitor except that the final result will appear in the balance of payments account.

Speculation is often in the form of selling for future rather than immediate settlement and is further discussed in Chapter 5.

If the rate of inflation of one country is growing at a rate which is different from another, then the prices of goods in the two countries will move at different rates. In order to bring them back into line it may be necessary to change the rate of exchange, as was mentioned at the beginning of the chapter. It is normal for the country with the higher rate of inflation to have to reduce (devalue) the price of its money relative to another. If both countries have the same rate of inflation, however high the figure, then it may not be necessary to reduce the price of its money. It is, therefore, important to watch such indices as the Retail Price or Wholesale Price Index.

Politics will also affect the rate of exchange in so far as a change of government from one with sound economic policies to one with proclaimed unsound economic, financial or monetary policies will immediately cause the rate of exchange to fall in anticipation of perhaps higher inflation, increased spending overseas, or reduced incentive for exporters. An unpopular government, with perhaps the threat of a civil war, would make a foreign holder of the currency nervous since this could lead to increased imports (arms), failing exports (business destroyed), inflation (limited goods), and again selling of a currency would begin.

Often the rate of exchange will move in anticipation of, rather than because of, an occurrence. This will often give rise to a contradictory movement in an exchange rate. If, for example, it was anticipated that a country would show a balance of payments deficit of $10 billion, then the exchange rate may well have moved to reflect this. If, however, the country still had a balance of payments deficit when it reported its figures but the amount was only $5 billion, then the currency might improve in value since the amount of the deficit was nowhere near that which had been anticipated. This movement would be contradictory to the theory that a currency with a negative balance of payments must reduce in value or devalue.

If there is foreknowledge of a large requirement for a particular currency for a particular day, or if two central banks have agreed to maintain a rate, or if a particular market-maker is taking a very special short-term view of a currency, a rate of exchange could change notwithstanding that the move is not the result of one of the more traditional causes.

FORWARD RATES OF EXCHANGE

In addition to buying or selling a currency for immediate or spot delivery, it is possible to buy and sell a currency for future delivery in exchange for the payment of another currency. This future exchange will take place on a specifically agreed business day in the future at a rate of exchange which has been fixed at the time the contract was consummated. It should be noted that, whilst the amount of the transaction, the value date and the exchange rate have all been determined in advance, *no* exchange of money takes place until the actual settlement date. Such transactions are called 'forward transactions'.

Forward transactions are either 'swaps' or 'outrights'. An outright is a forward purchase or sale of a currency at a foreign exchange rate which expresses the actual price of one currency against another for a specific value date. A swap is more complicated and is the purchase of one currency against another for one specific maturity date and the simultaneous reversal of that contract for another, different, maturity date. The difference between the two exchange rates in a swap is called the 'swap rate'.

To calculate a forward rate of exchange is perhaps best illustrated by way of Example 2.3.

EXAMPLE 2.3

A UK importer buys goods from the United States on 90-day credit terms. He is invoiced in US dollars. At the time of purchase, the spot exchange rate of US$2 = £1 prevails, the cost of borrowing 90 days sterling to a bank is 10 % p.a., and a bank can reinvest US dollars for 90 days at 7 % p.a. The importer can choose to cover his exchange risk in two ways, since he has to pay US dollars but will be receiving pounds:

1. Execute a spot foreign exchange transaction with the bank at $2 = £1.

   ∴ The customer has not yet been paid for goods by his buyers.

   Consequently, he has *no* sterling available to undertake the spot transaction and must, therefore, borrow from the bank who in turn must borrow the funds in the money market at 10 % p.a. The customer then undertakes conversion of pounds into US dollars. The US dollars are not, however, required for 90 days under the terms of sale so the bank will accept them on deposit for 90 days at 7 % p.a. At the maturity of the deposit, the funds will be used to pay the United States exporter.

2. Execute a forward foreign exchange transaction for settlement in 90 days' time at a given rate. Question – at what rate?

Spot rate = \$2 = £1
Cost to bank of borrowing sterling for 90 days = 10 % p.a.
Bank can reinvest US dollars for days at 7 % p.a.
∴ Difference in interest rates between the two currencies is 3 % p.a.
(interest rate differential).
∴ If the spot rate of exchange can be adjusted to reflect this loss of 3 % p.a., a forward rate of exchange could be obtained.

Method

Amount by which spot rate must be adjusted = Spot rate of exchange × interest rate differential

$$= \times \text{ period annualised}$$

$$= 2 \times \frac{3}{100} \times \frac{90}{360}$$

$$= .015$$

N.B. It is practice in the foreign exchange market to base most calculations on actual number of days but with 360 days in a year.

In Example 2.3, the spot rate must be adjusted by .015 but is it to be added to the number or subtracted from it? In the example, the bank borrows at 10 per cent p.a. but can only earn 7 per cent p.a. so it is, therefore, losing 3 per cent p.a. To put it another way, the cost to the bank is 3 per cent p.a.

If \$2 = £1 for immediate delivery, it should be more expensive to settle for future delivery in order to compensate for this 3 per cent p.a. loss:

$$∴ \$2 \text{ minus } .015 = £1$$
$$∴ \$1.985 = £1 = \text{outright rate of exchange}$$

In other words, each pound will only buy \$1.985 instead of \$2.

As previously mentioned, the amount by which the spot rate of exchange has been adjusted is called the 'swap rate' or 'forward differential' and in Example 2.3, because it is more expensive to buy US dollars for future delivery, the US dollar is said to be at a premium to the pound. Conversely, the pound is cheaper relative to the US dollar and is said to be at a discount.

It is necessary to be precise when discussing premiums and discounts since reference must be made to the currency, e.g. from the previous sentence, the pound is at a discount to the dollar but the dollar is at a premium to the pound. If in doubt as to whether to add or subtract the forward differential, then refer to the interest differential between the two currencies for the appropriate period and see if there is a cost or a profit to the bank were it to cover the transaction by lending and borrowing instead of by a forward contract. If a cost, then the forward rate should be more expensive relative to the spot rate; if a profit, then the forward rate should be cheaper relative to the spot rate. This is illustrated by Example 2.4.

EXAMPLE 2.4

	$/£	$/DM
Spot	1.9000 – 10	2.0000 – 25
1 month forward	20 – 30	30 – 25
3 months forward	5p – 5d	90 – 85

The above illustrates some typical quotes. The outright prices would be:

	$/£	$/DM
Spot rate	1.9000 – 1.9010	2.0000 – 2.0025
1 month forward	20 –　30	30 –　25
Forward outright rate	1.9020 – 1.9040	1.9970 – 2.0000

	$/£	$/DM
Spot rate	1.9000 – 1.9010	2.0000 – 2.0025
3 months forward	5p –　5d	90 –　85
Forward outright rate	1.8995 – 1.9015	1.9910 – 1.9940

Example 2.4 shows the pound at a discount to the dollar for the one-month rate, at a premium or discount to the dollar for the three-month rate, and the Deutschmark at a premium to the dollar for both one and three months. Therefore, sterling interest rates for one month maturities are lower than dollar rates and

about the same for three-month maturities. Deutschmark interest rates are all lower than dollar rates. Therefore, when discussing pounds relative to dollars or other currencies relative to the dollar, the rule is: if a premium, subtract from the spot rate; if a discount, add to the spot rate.

The basis of calculation for all forward rates of exchange or swap rates is the interest differential between the two currencies for a given period. The interest differential is the difference between the interest rates in the Euro-markets, which is not necessarily the same as the difference between the domestic interest rates of the two countries. For the foreign exchange transaction to occur, it must be possible to freely convert the currencies in question and to be able to lend and borrow them. Exchange controls, taxation, reserve requirements and other factors often affect domestic interest rates. Consequently, the domestic deposit rates are often lower than Euro-rates. Therefore, even if a spot rate of exchange moves upwards or downwards, it is not always necessary for the swap rate to alter. However, there will be occasions when the swap rate does not exactly equal the interest differential. At this time, arbitraging will take place until such time as the swap rate will exactly equal the interest differential. This is discussed in detail in Chapter 5.

In Example 2.3, the forward transaction was caused because an importer wished to ensure that no matter which way the spot rate of exchange moved, he had guaranteed his rate of exchange and so he could safely bill his customers knowing that his profit margin would be unaffected by a currency movement. This action of covering a foreign exchange exposure is called 'hedging'.

If a large number of people believe that a rate of exchange is liable to significant change during a specific period, then they will either hedge to protect themselves, as will the importer, or will hedge in expectation of making a profit. If all believe a currency is going to depreciate in value (devalue) relative to another, then there will be more sellers than buyers of the forward outrights. Under these conditions, a distortion between the interest differential swap rate and the actual rate will occur such that the forward rate becomes more expensive, i.e. the forward premium will increase.

When a spot rate of exchange depreciates, its swap rate or forward premium will normally increase. Conversely, when a spot rate of exchange appreciates, its swap rate will normally decrease. This is so since a currency which is liable to devalue is weak and the weakness may have occurred as a result of high inflation or because money is leaving the country for any number of reasons. As a means of trying to prevent this, a government may resort to increasing interest rates in order to make deposits in its currency appear more attractive. Hence, if the interest rates in one currency increase at a faster rate than another, the interest differential between the two will widen and so the swap rate will increase. If the interest differential narrows, the swap rate will be reduced. Using the formula which has already been discussed, Example 2.5 may help to clarify this.

EXAMPLE 2.5

(a) Assume interest differential between USA and UK for a one-year deposit is 3% p.a.
Spot rate of exchange: $2 = £1
$$\therefore \ \$2 \times \frac{3}{100} \times \frac{365}{360} = .06 = \text{swap rate}$$

(b) Interest differential now: 6% p.a.
No change in spot rate of exchange
$$\therefore \ \$2 \times \frac{6}{100} \times \frac{365}{360} = .12 = \text{swap rate}$$

(c) Interest differential now: 1% p.a.
No change in spot rate of exchange
$$\therefore \ \$2 \times \frac{1}{100} \times \frac{365}{360} = .02 = \text{swap rate}$$

Central banks use the forward foreign exchange market as a means of supporting their currencies. This can also cause distortions. The method and purpose of their intervention is more fully discussed in Chapter 10. It should also be remembered that most transactions in the foreign exchange markets are for maturities of under six months. Therefore, if a transaction in excess of six months is contemplated, the price of the outright contract may be more expensive relative to the interest rate differential in order to protect the bank against the additional risks caused by the relative thinness of the foreign exchange market.

In a fixed-parity system of foreign exchange, the movement of the spot rate of exchange is limited around the agreed par value. No such limitation applies to the forward rate of exchange. In a floating-exchange system, all are free to move. Chapter 1 mentioned the snake of the EEC: this is a type of fixed-rate parity system for certain currencies relative to each other. Therefore, even here it is only the spot rates of exchange which are controlled, not the forward rates.

Spot and forward rates of exchange are, therefore, linked. They move for similar reasons with the exception that the dominant influence on forward rates of exchange is the interest differential.

3 The Dealing Theory of Deposits

Alongside the foreign exchange market is the money market or deposit market. As has been mentioned in the preceding chapter, there is an interaction between the two markets. Since the money markets are larger in size than the foreign exchange markets, the influence of interest rates on the foreign exchange market tends to be more important than the exchange rates on the money market.

Whereas in the foreign exchange market one currency is expressed as being worth so many units of another, in the deposit market the prices are normally expressed in terms of percentage rates per annum—the interest rate. Interest can be defined as either the payment for the use of the money or the reward for parting with liquidity. The definition to be used depends upon one being either a lender or a borrower of the money.

The amount of interest is normally paid by the borrower to the lender in one of three ways:

1. *At Maturity of the Loan* In the professional money markets, this is probably the most common. Here funds are lent or placed on deposit for a given period at a given rate of interest, for example:

$1,000,000 is lent for one year at 10 per cent per annum. $1,000,000 is paid to the borrower at the beginning of the loan and $1,000,000 plus $100,000 interest $\left(1,000,000 \times \dfrac{10}{100} \text{ p.a.} \right)$ is repaid at maturity.

2. *At the Beginning of the Loan* This method of paying interest at the commencement of the loan or deposit is called 'discounting'.

It is widely used in trade transactions involving Bills of Exchange, for example:

A $1,000,000 Bill of Exchange is sold by the holder to the lender at a discount rate of 10% p.a. The Bill matures in one year.

$1,000,000 *less* the discount of $100,000 $\left(1,000,000 \times \dfrac{10}{100} \text{ p.a.} \right)$ paid to the borrower at the beginning of the loan.

$1,000,000 is *however* paid by the borrower to the lender at the maturity of the loan. Therefore, the effective rate or true cost of this loan is higher than in the previous example since the borrower only received $900,000 at the beginning compared with $1,000,000 in the previous example, but is effectively paying the same amount of interest. Therefore, the effective cost is 11.11% p.a.

$$(\$900,000 \times \frac{\textit{Effective Cost}}{100} \times 1 \text{ year} = \$100,000$$
$$\text{Effective Cost} = 11.11\% \text{ p.a.})$$

3. *At Intervals during the Life of the Loan* This method of paying interest is generally used if the maturity of the loan or deposit is in excess of one year or if the balance is liable to fluctuation. The amount of interest is calculated at regular intervals. In such cases, the effective rate of interest is higher than the actual rate, for example:

$1,000,000 is lent for one year at 10% p.a. interest to be paid semi-annually. Therefore interest for the whole year amounts to $100,000 as in 1. above, but this time it will be paid in two semi-annual instalments of $50,000 each time, so effective cost is 10.25% p.a. (10% p.a. is actual rate +cost of providing $50,000 for six months, assuming same actual rate of 10% p.a.)

THE DETERMINATION OF INTEREST RATES

Interest has been defined as the payment for the use of the money and as the reward for parting with liquidity. This payment of interest will, therefore, vary with time. The longer the period of time, then the higher should be the reward to the lender since the lender will need to be compensated for his loss of liquidity. A lender will, therefore, always try to obtain the highest reward for the use of his money whilst ensuring that the loan will be repaid, i.e. rate versus risk. A borrower will always try to obtain the funds at the cheapest price—the lowest rate of interest—and will not borrow the funds unless he believes that, notwithstanding the rate of interest, he can still use the borrowed money to obtain an even better return, thereby enabling him to make a profit even after the payment of interest.

The lowest interest rate which is paid for a particular period is normally the rate being paid by the government to obtain its money. This is often considered to be the best risk obtainable provided the borrowing is in the local or national currency. A government borrower is considered, in the local market, to be a near riskless borrower. If a borrower is of lesser quality, then a lender will usually require that a higher rate of interest be paid in order to be compensated for accepting the higher risk of repayment.

As in most economics, it is supply and demand which determine a price: so it is in determining an interest rate. Not only does a government create the demand, it can also influence the supply of money. Therefore, if the government allows the money supply to increase, rates of interest should decrease. This must not be taken as an axiom since if supply increases, money loses in value, inflation increases, and demand for credit can occur since people will try to buy now and borrow rather than save and pay later at the higher price. To reduce the demand, a government may increase the cost of borrowing to make it less attractive and so regain control of the interest rate structure.

In the Euro-markets, there are three other factors which determine interest rates. Firstly, the Euro-market is usually free of any reserve requirements compared with a domestic market. For example, in the United States, Regulation D of the Federal Reserve System determines the amount of reserves which must be provided against various types of deposit. Also in the United States, all small deposits are insured by the Federal Deposit Insurance Corporation (FDIC), in exchange for which the bank pays a premium. Therefore, in order to compare a Euro-rate with a domestic rate, the FDIC premium must be considered together with Regulation M of the Federal Reserve System which determines the amount of reserves which must be paid when an offshore deposit is used onshore in the United States. Therefore:

Domestic US Rate of Interest +
Reserve Cost + FDIC Premium   = Cost of Deposit
Euro-dollar Rate of Interest +
Regulation M   = Cost of Euro-deposit in USA

If there is no other constraint on the movement of money, such as exchange control, money will flow into or out of the United States until the two rates are equal. Because of this, Euro-rates are often higher than the domestic rates of interest since a Euro-Interest Rate is equal to the Domestic Interest Rate *plus* the cost of reserves, etc.

Exchange control is the second factor which can determine interest rates. If money cannot move freely between the Euro-market and the domestic market, as, for example, in the case of sterling or French francs, then artificial demand and supply can occur. For instance, during the sterling crisis of 1967/8, pounds were being sold and other currencies purchased. The main purchaser of the sterling was the Bank of England and many of the sellers were non-residents of the United Kingdom. Because banks in the United Kingdom are restricted by exchange control in lending sterling overseas, it meant that the domestic market had an adequate supply of funds, whereas the Euro-sterling deposit market was short of funds which could not be borrowed except from a non-resident. Therefore, there was a very wide disparity of interest rates, often as high as 30–40 per cent p.a.

The third factor is the exchange rate. If a currency is about to be revalued then, as already discussed, buyers will exceed sellers. Once the buyer has purchased the currency to be revalued by selling another currency which has probably been borrowed, he will wish to earn a return on the currency now held. As more buyers appear so, therefore, will more lenders of the currency to be revalued. An excess of supply will occur and interest rates will fall.

All of the above is true no matter which markets are being compared. However, when comparing the United States domestic market with the Euro-market, there is one other factor to be considered—Regulation Q of the Federal Reserve Board.

Regulation Q limits the rate of interest which a United States commercial bank can pay on certain domestic deposits in the USA. If this rate of interest is reached and the commercial bank needs funds, it can increase the demand for money in another centre since it is not limited in the rate of interest which it can pay to obtain deposits outside the USA. Therefore, in periods of tight money, it is not just a question of which is the cheapest market but a question of where the funds are available. This will inevitably lead to an increase in the deposit rates of interest in the Euro-market.

THE YIELD CURVE

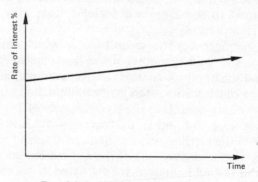

FIG. 3.1 A typical normal yield curve

Figure 3.1 illustrates a normal yield curve. The longer the maturity, the higher the interest rate demanded. There are also two other types of graph:

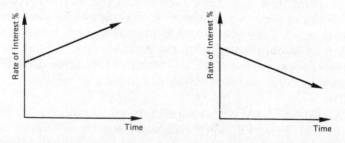

FIG. 3.2 Rising interest rates

FIG. 3.3 Falling interest rates

If the interest rates are expected to rise, then Figure 3.2 will apply, since there will be an increased demand for deposits of a longer maturity as borrowers will try to ensure that funds are obtained for as long as possible at the cheapest rate. Also, some speculation will occur in that funds will be borrowed at the low rate before they are actually required and will then be placed on deposit until needed. Thus there will be an increased demand for long-term funds and an increased supply of short-term funds.

Figure 3.3 will apply if it is expected that interest rates are about to decline. Lenders will lend, for as long as they consider prudent, in anticipation that the money must be lent whilst the return is still attractive and available, thereby increasing the supply of long-term funds. Borrowers will prefer to borrow for as short a period as possible in the expectation that, at the maturity of the loan, it will be cheaper to refinance. Speculation of falling rates will, therefore, lead to an increased demand for loans of shorter maturities and an increased supply of longer-term funds.

In practice, money markets are often a combination of all three graphs depending upon the time-scale involved, and a 'U' curve is created.

TYPES OF DEPOSIT

In the money markets, there are three types of deposit:

1. *Clean* A clean deposit is the payment by one party to another of funds without any conditions attached. The majority of money market transactions are of this type. The lender accepts no security for the placement of the deposit since the transaction is between two mutually satisfactory counterparties.

2. *Secured* Against the placement of the deposit, the lender accepts as collateral some form of security often equal to, or in excess of, the amount of the deposit. This is often found in money markets where it is customary for the deposit to be evidenced by a negotiable piece of paper. In such markets, some of the participants may not be banks and as a precaution the bank takes the negotiable document as collateral in the event that the counterparty is unable to repay the deposit. Examples of this are the London Discount Market, the New York Certificate of Deposit Market and the French Discount Market.

3. *Negotiable* Money market deposits are usually made for a fixed amount, at a fixed rate, for a specific period. Whilst this might appear to be acceptable to the lender and borrower at the

commencement of the deposit, it may not be acceptable to the lender at a later date because of, for example, a change in the lender's liquidity, a change in interest rates, or a change in the borrower's financial condition. To overcome these types of problem, two solutions are possible: either the borrower exceptionally allows repayment at an earlier date, or some other lender has to be found in place of the original lender. The techniques of negotiability have long been used by borrowers: governments have issued Treasury Bills and Bonds; merchants have issued Bills of Exchange. However, it was not until the 1960s that banks began to use it for deposits. An instrument called a Certificate of Deposit was created which enabled both parties to overcome their problems.

A Certificate of Deposit is a negotiable instrument in bearer form issued by a bank to certify that a specified sum has been deposited with the issuing bank at a stated rate of interest to be repaid on a specified day. The rate of interest will normally be the same for all of the period in question but it is possible to have a variable interest rate which is adjusted at predetermined intervals such as every six months during the life of the Certificate of Deposit.

4 Objectives, Organisation and Operation of a Dealing Department

Banks are the intermediary in the money system in so far as they accept deposits, either demand or time, interest-bearing or non-interest bearing, from customers and then use these deposits to make loans, or other deposits with other banks, or to purchase investments. At the same time, they are the intermediary in international trade since they enable their financial and commercial customers to buy and sell the foreign exchange which they require. The banks also enable their customers to invest their surplus funds in foreign currency deposits with them. The objectives of the dealing department are to satisfy these needs in a satisfactory manner for both customer and banker.

OBJECTIVES

A dealing department is composed of two types of interrelated business: Money Market and Foreign Exchange. These two have to work together since, as has already been discussed, the markets are effectively connected.

What, then, are the objectives of a dealing department?

(a) To control the liquidity and foreign exchange exposure of the bank.
(b) To provide a service to satisfy the customer's needs.
(c) To produce a profit to the bank.

Banks receive deposits from a variety of sources for varying periods. It is the responsibility of the dealing department to ensure that any excess funds are invested where they will produce the highest return to the bank. However, prudence, management,

31

local regulations etc. will have placed limits on how and where such excess funds are invested since it is imperative that the solvency and liquidity of the bank are maintained.

Should a bank not have excess funds for a given period, then it is the responsibility of the dealing department to borrow and thereby obtain these funds in the cheapest manner. This may necessitate borrowing the funds in one currency and then converting them through the foreign exchange market into the currency required.

Commercial banks have customers who buy foreign exchange from them and customers who sell foreign exchange to them. To facilitate the handling of such transactions, the commercial bank will maintain accounts in a variety of foreign currencies with either their overseas branches and affiliates or with other banks. Such accounts are called 'nostro' or 'due from' accounts. Balances will be left in these accounts: such balances represent a foreign exchange exposure to the bank and a loss of interest. However, it is not just these balances which make up the foreign exchange position of a bank. Such a position comprises:

(a) Surplus foreign exchange balances.
(b) ± difference between outstanding foreign exchange contracts for both spot and forward delivery.
(c) ± difference between interest to be received in a foreign currency and interest to be paid away in the same foreign currency.
(d) Possible foreign currency capital exposure in an affiliate or branch if it has not been covered by a foreign currency borrowing or a forward exchange contract.
(e) Other payables or receivables in foreign currencies such as taxes due, fees, dividends to be received, etc.

The dealing department has to monitor the total of (a), (b), (c), (d) and (e) in order to ensure that the total foreign exchange position of the bank is known. It will then, in conjunction with management, determine what will be a prudent level for such exposure, taking into consideration the size of the bank, the volatility of the exchange markets, the profit or loss exposure and whether or not local exchange control regulations of the central bank will permit such an exposure.

To provide a service to a customer's needs means ensuring that the customer is given the best possible advice or quotation for a transaction. The money and foreign exchange markets are very competitive. Therefore, a dealing department must be responsive to the customer's requirements. For example, if a customer has funds to place on deposit for a particular period, the dealing room should try to pay the customer a competitive rate of interest since the bank, not just the dealing room, will otherwise lose the customer to a rival bank. The same would be true for a foreign exchange transaction, where a firm competitive quote is required, otherwise another bank will perform the transaction and gain the customer.

Customers expect their banks, and in particular their dealing departments, to provide them with counsel as to the probable movement of an exchange rate or the possibility of a change in interest rates. Banks which provide sound advice are appreciated by their customers for it assists them in their business decisions and enables them to be profitable. Often this can be as important in retaining a customer as a competitive quotation.

All of this activity is designed to produce a profit to the bank for, unless this is so, it would be questionable if this is a worthwhile exercise. Whilst later chapters will show in detail how the profits are made, mention should perhaps be made of from where the profits will come.

The largest source of income to a bank is normally the difference between the rates of interest paid for the deposits and the rates of interest earned from the loans. This is either called the 'spread' or 'interest differential'. The interest differential between the assets and liabilities managed by the dealing department is, therefore, a primary source of profit. Profit will also come from exchange rate differences. The price paid when a foreign currency is purchased is, hopefully, lower than the price obtained upon its sale. Income will come from fees and commissions charged by the bank in exchange for services rendered to the customer. Float, or the use of interest-free balances, can also generate income if the amount is larger than the idle balances which a bank keeps on its nostro accounts. If a bank buys and sells negotiable instruments, then this too can generate a profit.

Offsetting part of this income are the expenses associated with staffing and processing the transactions. Nevertheless, a dealing department should, and must, be considered as a profit centre. Figure 4.1 is perhaps typical of the organisation of a dealing

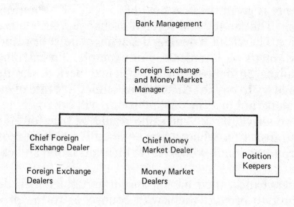

FIG. 4.1 Organisation chart

department. The number of people involved and the number of other subdivisions will depend upon the size of the bank, its level of activity and the country in which it is located. Also, the level of computerisation will affect in particular the number of position keepers.

Management of a bank looks to the foreign exchange and money market manager to achieve the objectives already described, and it is up to this manager to ensure that these objectives are implemented. To ensure that the dealing policy is uniform, it is becoming increasingly common for an overall foreign exchange and treasury manager to be located in the head office. Whilst the organisation chart shows the money market and foreign exchange dealers as separate, it is vital that in practice they work closely together as a team. There is at all times so much interaction between exchange rates and interest rates that both groups must be continually aware of what is happening in the other's market since it will probably have a very direct effect on their market.

Within a dealing department, the numbers and types of specialist will vary depending upon the size of the bank and its level of involvement in the markets. However, many trading departments have specialist dealers for their own local currency foreign exchange transactions, for their local currency treasury and for customer transactions.

If the bank is an active participant in the market, further

subdivision may occur and the foreign exchange dealers may specialise even further by, for example, some specialising in a particular currency, others in spot trading or in forward trading. Similarly, a bank may have treasury and money market specialists for a particular currency or for deposits up to maturities of seven days, whilst there may be further dealers responsible for maturities in excess of seven days.

A bank will often have dealers specialising in a particular type of customer – for example, central banks, oil companies, other branches, etc.—and these can either be a third group of dealers or a part of one of the two groups. Some banks specialise in other activities such as banknote dealing, bullion and precious metal dealing, negotiable asset dealing, etc. No matter how diverse the activity or how many people are involved, all must work together as a team since profit opportunities can occur by arbitraging between the various markets, and if the dealers act as individuals, such opportunities will be missed.

The third group in the dealing department is the position keepers. Their job may be manual or handled by computer, but the principle is the same—to record the currency exposure of the bank or dealing department; to see the dealers are informed if they are over-bought, over-sold, over-lent or over-borrowed in a particular currency. Their role is vital since the foreign exchange manager must be aware of the position or exposure at any moment in time in order to be able to determine how the rates are to be quoted by the dealing department.

In some banks, the position maintained in the dealing room is not the same as the total bank position as previously described since some banks exclude from the dealing department responsibility for long-term capital exposure. Also, unless the dealers have the benefit of a computer system, it is doubtful whether the dealer position will reflect all the foreign exchange exposure resulting, for example, from interest payments.

OPERATION OF A DEALING DEPARTMENT

The manager or senior dealer will, in consultation with the bank's management and dealers, determine each day what type and level of position the bank should hold. The dealing team will note what has happened in other dealing centres around the world and will then adjust their rates of exchange and rates for deposits based on these factors. They will also ascertain whether any political or economic news has been published which might in some way affect a currency or change a rate.

As the day progresses, the rates will move depending upon the type of business being conducted and market trends. If the bank is a major participant in the foreign and treasury markets, then it will, in all probability, be an active day. If, on the other hand, the bank is not a major market maker, then probably it will only deal to the extent necessary to satisfy customers' requirements. Thus, it will contact a major trader, execute the order, and then pass the price or rate received on to the customer after deducting some commission for completing the transaction.

A dealer will usually transact the business in one of several ways: by telephone; by telex; through a broker; by cable or other written instruction. Upon receipt of the order, the dealer will make a quotation. If the quotation is accepted by the counterparty, a deal is made.

RECORDING A DEAL

A deal must be recorded in the books of the bank, confirmed to the customer and processed so that payment of the money will occur. To initiate the recording of the transaction, a dealer will usually complete a pre-printed form known as a deal ticket or voucher. Whilst the format of the ticket varies from bank to bank, the information to be recorded should include the following if it is a foreign exchange deal:

(a) The name of the counterparty or customer.
(b) The location of the counterparty.
(c) The date of the transaction—the contract date.
(d) The value date of the transaction.
(e) The currency and amount purchased.
(f) The currency and amount sold.
(g) The rate of exchange at which the transaction has been consummated.
(h) Designation if deal is for spot or forward delivery.
(i) Settlement instructions: To where the monies sold are to be paid.
　　　　　　　　　　　　　How the money bought is to be received.

(j) Name of broker if applicable.
(k) Signature or initials of dealer to confirm the transaction and to use if necessary for accountability.

It may well be that the dealer will only partly complete the ticket and that the operations department will complete the missing information. For example, a computer system will calculate the amount of the equivalent currency provided it is informed of the currency and amount of the deal, the exchange rate and the denomination of the equivalent currency. The settlement instructions might need to be agreed at a later date or the address might need to be verified.

Once the ticket has been completed by the dealer, it will be passed to the position keeper who will either manually, or by inputting into a computer, record the transaction as to the value date, the rate, the name of the customer, the currency and amount bought and sold. In this way, the position is updated.

From here, the ticket is passed to the operations department or servicing department. For reasons of control, this is often not the responsibility of the dealing department. The operations department will:

(a) Complete the dealing ticket.
(b) Ascertain the method of settlement.
(c) See a confirmation is prepared and sent to the customer – this is called the contract.
(d) Prepare the entries for book-keeping and accounting.
(e) See that the telexes sent to effect the payment are correct.
(f) Check the incoming confirmation from the customer and /or broker to see that all parties agree as to the terms of the transaction.
(g) If a forward transaction, ensure that a duplicate contract is sent as a reminder nearer to the value date.
(h) Maintain a duplicate position sheet.
(i) Ensure that foreign currency nostro accounts have sufficient funds to effect the payment.
(j) Maintain files of all transactions in the event of a query or audit.
(k) Produce such management reports as are necessary.

If the transaction is a money market transaction, whilst the process is essentially the same, the deal ticket will require different information. Therefore, for a deposit transaction, the ticket should include:

(a) The name of the counterparty.
(b) The location of the counterparty.
(c) The date of the transaction—the contract date.
(d) The start-date of the deposit—the value date.
(e) The maturity date of the deposit.
(f) The currency and amount lent or borrowed.
(g) The rate of interest at which the transaction has been consummated.
(h) Settlement instructions – to where and how funds are to be paid at the beginning and at the maturity of the deposit.
(i) Designation—if the deal is a loan or a deposit.
(j) Name of broker if applicable.
(k) Signature or initials of dealer to confirm the transaction and to use, if necessary, for accountability.

The positioning and operations department procedure is then very similar. An accurate accounting system for the transaction is essential. Such a system must be capable of:

(a) Listing all contracts with a particular customer.
(b) Listing all contracts for a particular day.
(c) Producing accurate position records, both spot and forward, for dealers and management.
(d) Producing profit and loss figures for the dealing department—both foreign exchange and interest.
(e) Producing such statutory reports as are necessary to ensure that the bank at all times complies with local exchange control regulations.
(f) Producing reports to ensure that the dealing department is adhering to management guidelines
(g) Daily projection of movements in nostro accounts.

Much of the above information is initiated with the preparation of the Contract Confirmation. This is often a multi-carbon form with sufficient copies to create all the necessary input information for either the manual or computer accounting system at the outset of the deal. In other systems, the information on the trading voucher is entered directly into the computer system through a keyboard.

No matter which system is used, a contract must be produced, checked, and usually verified before mailing to the customer. To summarise, it may be useful to consider the following flow chart:

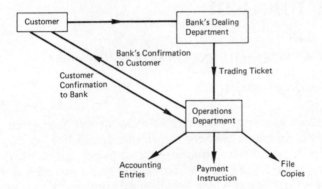

FIG. 4.2 Flow chart for typical deal

PAYMENT

Payments and receipts for the dealing department are made in accordance with normal banking practice, i.e. by telex, direct debits or credits, transmission of computer data, cheque or bankers' payments. However, it is essential for the dealing department to be informed of any errors or fails as they will affect their money position. Thus, a copy of all payment telexes is normally sent to the servicing or operations department for verification. Also, a correspondent bank is often informed of monies which are expected so that, in the event of their non-receipt the dealing department can cover the position until the funds are received.

5 Practice of the Dealing Function

PART A. FOREIGN EXCHANGE

QUOTATIONS

In previous chapters, whenever an example has been given, just one rate of exchange has been mentioned. In practice, whenever a dealer is requested for a quotation, two prices will be provided. The first price is the one at which he will buy a currency and the second is the price at which he will sell a currency. For example:

EXAMPLE 5.1

$$\$/\pounds \qquad 1.8320–1.8325$$
$$\$/DM \qquad 2.0530–2.0545$$

Using the above rates, in the first case either £1000 = $1832.00 or £1000 = $1832.50. Therefore, if a dealer is being asked to purchase £1000 and to sell the equivalent amount of currency, the deal will be done at 1.8320 since the dealer only has to part with $1832, *not* $1832.50. If, however, the dealer is being asked to sell sterling then in exchange the dealer would wish to obtain as many dollars as possible. Therefore, the deal is done at $1.8325.

The second case—$/DM—would work in exactly the same way. If a dealer is buying $1000 then in exchange he would wish to part with as few Deutschmarks as possible, i.e. DM2053.00. If selling $1000, the dealer would receive DM2054.50.

The choice of the rates favours the market-maker or the one being asked. Obviously one person's selling price is the other's buying price. Therefore, it is essential to realise that the dealer sometimes has to deal on the wrong side of the price since he is not the market-maker but the customer wishing to transact a deal. In foreign exchange there are always two currencies involved since the meaning of foreign exchange is the conversion of one currency into another.

Example 5.1 illustrates how in the case of sterling it is quoted as £1 = so many dollars, and in the case of $/DM it is quoted as $1 = so many Deutschmarks. This is market convention. Therefore, in the case of the pound the rule is, one pound is quoted as being worth so many foreign currency units. Similarly, outside the USA the convention is $1 = so many units of a foreign currency. This is contrary to the method of direct quotations which means that in France, for example, foreign currencies are expressed in terms of French francs; in Holland in terms of Dutch guilders, etc. Within the United States, and sometimes in Europe or the Far East, a quotation may be expressed as one foreign unit being equal to so many local units. This is called an 'indirect quotation'. Therefore, to rationalise the rule: if quoting against the pound or US dollar, it is the number of foreign units which equal one pound or one dollar; for other currencies, the direct method prevails.

In practice, if a professional dealer is speaking to another professional dealer, the quotation would rarely be 1.8320–1.8325 but would be expressed as 20–25, it being assumed that the other party was aware of the principal figures as an active participant in the markets. However, with such recent volatility in the market, it is never wrong to check the whole price if in doubt.

Because of the importance of the US dollar in world trade, it is the practice that all currencies are expressed or quoted against the US dollar since if this rate is known, other rates can be calculated.

To revert to Example 5.1: $/£ = 1.8320 − 1.8325; $/DM = 2.0530 − 2.0545. Using these rates, it is possible to calculate the rate of exchange for sterling/Deutschmarks. This is called a 'cross-rate' and is calculated as follows:

EXAMPLE 5.2

£1 = $1.8320 (The dealer's buying rate for pounds and selling rate for US dollars as the

£1 = $1.8325 (The dealer's selling rate for pounds and buying rate for US dollars as the

market-maker)
$1 = DM2.0530
(The dealer's rate for selling Deutschmarks and for buying US dollars as the market-maker)

market-maker)
$1 = DM2.0545
(The dealer's rate for buying Deutschmarks and for selling US dollars as the market-maker)

Therefore, the rate at which a dealer will buy pounds and sell Deutschmarks can be calculated by taking the buying rate for pounds and the selling rate for dollars and the selling rate for Deutschmarks and the buying rate for dollars.

∴ To calculate rate for DM/£ using above rates:

£1 = $1.8320   In cover, dealer can buy dollars and sell pounds at this rate in the market.

$1 = DM2.0530   In cover, dealer can sell dollars and buy Deutschmarks at this rate in the market.

$$\therefore \text{ also } \$1 = \frac{1}{1.8320} \text{ pounds}$$

$$\therefore \text{ DM2.0530} = \frac{1}{1.8320} \text{ pounds}$$

$$\therefore \text{ DM2.0530} \times 1.8320 = 1 \text{ pound}$$
$$\text{DM3.7610} = 1 \text{ pound}$$

To the customer, the dealer is the market-maker; but in covering, the dealer will in all probability not be the market-maker.

If it is desired to obtain a mid-rate for Deutschmarks against French francs, the principle is the same as Example 5.2 but the method of calculation differs because of the manner in which these two currencies are quoted:

EXAMPLE 5.3

Mid-point of $/DM from Example 5.2 is:

$$\frac{2.0530 + 2.0545}{2} = \text{DM2.05375} = \$1$$

Let us assume that the mid-point for dollars against francs is $1 = FFcs 4.50.

∴ To find how many FFcs = DM1
DM2.05375 = $1
$1 = FFcs 4.50

$$\therefore \quad DM2.05375 = FFcs\ 4.50$$

$$\therefore \quad DM1 = \frac{4.50}{2.05375}$$

$$= FFcs\ 2.1911$$

Convention would then be for the rate to be expressed as DM100 = FFcs 219.11 since it is usual for 100 units of a currency to be used.

VALUE DATES

The foreign exchange rates which have been used in Example 5.1–3 are spot rates of exchange. This means that transactions entered into today will be settled between the two contracting parties, two business or working days later. Because two currencies are involved, it must be a day on which the two currencies can be exchanged. Therefore, by way of an example, a spot deal contracted on a Wednesday will be settled on a Friday; a spot deal contracted on a Thursday will be settled on a Monday since banks in the major money markets of New York, London, Paris, Frankfurt and Zurich are closed over a weekend and settlement cannot take place. If a dollar/Swiss franc spot deal has been arranged on Thursday and if the following Monday is a public holiday in New York but not in Zurich, the transaction will not be settled nor funds exchanged until the Tuesday, when both centres are once again open. On the other hand, if a pound/Swiss franc transaction were concluded on the same Thursday, the spot date could be the Monday since the fact that New York closed for business would not affect this transaction. All foreign exchange transactions are calculated relative to the spot date. Therefore, if it is necessary to deal for value today or value tomorrow, and provided that this is not normal local market practice, a special quotation will have to be calculated relative to the spot date.

This two-day grace period between contract date and settlement date, when the monies are actually exchanged, is required so that all the administration and accounting which has been described in the previous chapter can be completed and checked. Also, because settlement will in all probability be occurring in two different countries, telexes will have to be sent to instruct the payments to be made. This is further complicated by the fact that different time-zones may be involved, e.g. a deal transacted in

New York late one day involving the selling of yen in Japan and the buying of Swiss francs in Zurich. If settlement were immediate it would be impossible as banks in Japan and Zurich would not be open for business. Cheques and mail transfers can be used but this can lead to uncertainty as to the exact value date.

Forward or futures trading and deposit or money market dealing also use the spot system to calculate the rate applicable for the period in question.

POSITION-TAKING

In the previous chapter, reference is made to the bank's position in foreign exchange. This section is concerned with the dealer's position. If a dealer is over-bought in a currency then the dealer is said to be 'long' or to have a 'long position'. If a dealer is over-sold in a currency then he is said to be 'short' or to have a 'short position'.

Because two currencies are always involved in any exchange transaction—one being bought, the other being sold—two positions are being affected, not one. As already mentioned, a position comprises the sum of the dealer's nostro balances, the difference between the forward purchases and sales in a currency, various payables and receivables and possibly, depending upon the bank, the inclusion of long-term capital in foreign currency. For example:

EXAMPLE 5.4

A bank's dealing department has no foreign currency positions at the beginning of a day. Let us see how a position is created, used and closed (+ = long, − = short):

First Deal	*Position*	
	US$	*DM*
Bank buys $1,000,000 from an oil client and sells Deutschmarks at 2.00 value spot.	+ 1,000,000	− 2,000,000

Second Deal

Bank buys $500,000 from another bank and sells Deutschmarks at 2.00 value spot.	+ 500,000	− 1,000,000
Dealer Foreign Exchange Position	+ 1,500,000	− 3,000,000

The bank has thus far been the market-maker and to effect the above transactions had quoted 2.00–2.01. If this is still the market price then to reduce the position to nil, the first dealer (A) would have to call another dealer (B) and sell the $1,500,000 and buy the Deutschmark equivalent at dealer B's price of 2.00 since dealer A is dealer B's customer. This would not result in any profit or loss to dealer A.

An alternative would be for dealer A to change the dealing price to 1.995–2.0050. If the rest of the market is still quoting 2.00–2.01 then dealer A's quotation is more attractive to a customer who wishes to buy US dollars since for every $1 the customer only has to give away DM2.005, compared with the rest of the market where the customer would have to give up DM2.01. On the other hand, dealer A's price of 1.995–2.0050 is not so attractive if the customer is a seller of US dollars because only DM1.995 will be given in exchange instead of DM2 which would be available from the rest of the market. Dealer A is, therefore, trying to find a buyer of US dollars against Deutschmarks, not another seller.

Third Deal	*Position*	
	US$	*DM*
b/f	+ 1,500,000	− 3,000,000
Bank sells $750,000 to another bank and buys Deutschmarks at 2.0050 value spot	− 750,000	+ 1,503,750
Net Dealer Foreign Exchange Position	+ 750,000	− 1,496,250

Dealer A now has a long or over-bought position at an exchange rate of 1.9950. If the rest of the market is still 2.00–2.01 $/DM then dealer A can again call dealer B for a quotation and this time dealer A can sell $750,000 at 2.00 to dealer B thereby receiving in exchange DM1,500,000 for value spot.

			Position	
Fourth Deal				
		US$	*DM*	
b/f		+ 750,000	− 1,496,250	
Bank does above deal with dealer B		− 750,000	+ 1,500,000	
Net Dealer Foreign Exchange Position		−	+ 3,750	

Therefore, on these deals, the bank has made a profit of DM3,750.

Example 5.4 is typical of how a position is created, traded and closed. In reality, a bank's dealer position comprises many such transactions against numerous currencies. Example 5.4 also shows why dealer A's prices differ from dealer B's—a different position was held. This is important because it is one of the reasons why there are different prices in the market at any particular time. Dealers may have large or small positions which may be either over-bought or over-sold in any one particular currency.

SPOT DEALING

A market-maker in foreign exchange normally bases the opening or beginning rates each day on the closing rates in the preceding time-zone. These rates may then be adjusted if conditions have changed which necessitate price alteration because of some new or anticipated item of economic or other news. The market-maker will then test the rates to see if they are good. A call will be made to another market-maker and a request made as to what their quotations are for spot transactions. If they agree, the term 'parity' will be used indicating that both agree. If the rates differ then a trade will, or could, occur since it is possible to commence a position at a better than indicated rate.

Markets are not free to move completely as they wish because central banks need to stabilise and at times influence the exchange rates. Also there are agreements limiting the range of movement for a currency: such were discussed in Chapter 1— Bretton Woods, the Smithsonian, the EEC 'snake'. These can provide dealers with profit opportunities. For example:

EXAMPLE 5.5

if $/DM = 2.1200 $/DFls = 2.2500

EEC Snake (1974)

DM/guilder

	Upper limit	DFls 101.885
DM100 =	Mid-Point	DFls 104.202
	Lower Point	DFls 106.56

From the previous formula, the cross-rate in the market of DM/DFls, using the above dollar rates, is DM100 = DFls 106.13. This rate is near the lower limit. Now, if the $/DM rate of 2.1200 does not change and the snake lower limit price is DM100 = DFls 106.56 then the $/DFls rate must not become stronger than DFls 2.2590 = $1. Therefore, if the dealer is able to buy Dutch florins at 2.2650 then a profit is guaranteed since if the EEC snake is to be preserved and if the $/DM rate does not change, the central bank must intervene to bring the market price back to 2.2590. At this point the dealer sells and makes a profit. Similarly, a position can be maintained in Deutschmarks against guilders secure in the knowledge that so long as the snake is preserved, there is a guaranteed lower intervention price to protect the dealer's position.

Profits can also be made in spot dealing by the simultaneous buying and selling between different counterparties in the same or different centres to take advantage of price differences. This is called 'arbitraging' or 'jobbing'. It is probably one of the most usual ways of making a profit. Sometimes it is possible because of different market practices. For example:

EXAMPLE 5.6

In Frankfurt: $/DM = 2.1008–16
In New York: DM/$ = .4750–.4760
i.e. $1 = DM2.1008 or $1 = DM2.1016 in Frankfurt
DM1 = $.4760 or DM1 = .4750 in New York

Frankfurt is quoting the direct way and New York the indirect way. To calculate the New York rate is, or should be, the reciprocal of the European (in this case Frankfurt) quote. Therefore, using the above:

(a) $\dfrac{1}{2.1008}$ = .4760 = rate for buying dollars and selling Deutschmarks.

(b) $\dfrac{1}{2.1016}$ = .4758 = rate for selling dollars and buying Deutschmarks.

In this case, rate (a) is identical in both the markets but rate (b) is different.

So, in Frankfurt the bank buys $2,000,000 at 2.1016 and sells DM4,203,200 (deal is done on other bank's terms as first bank is now the customer). In New York the bank sells $2,000,000 at .4750 and buys DM4,210,526.30. Therefore, a profit has been made of DM7326.30 because the rates had moved out of line with each other by .0008. This is called an eight-point difference. The fourth place after the decimal is called a point and the fifth, a pip. It is doubtful if such a situation would last for long as the two rates would move into line as more business was transacted.

The differing types of spot dealing in Examples 5.5 and 5.6 are of an offensive nature, i.e. the bank's dealing department wanted to trade and was searching for a profit opportunity. Sometimes it is wise to deal defensively.

In a very active and volatile market with prices continually changing, the market rate of exchange can move suddenly and what seemed to be a certain profit can become a certain loss. To obviate this problem a dealer will often widen the spread of the quotation, either to avoid dealing or in the event that a deal is done, to ensure that a reasonable chance of obtaining a profit exists. For example:

EXAMPLE 5.7

> Market: $/DM 2.1010–15 (narrow spread)
> $/DM 2.1000–30 (wide spread)

If the trader deals, a profit should result because the margin between bid and offer has been increased.

Finally, dealers will often try, under normal market conditions, to improve their dealing prices, i.e. to narrow the spread between bid and offer in order to obtain the business and the feel of the market. If a trader does not know the way of the market or cannot anticipate the trend, it is unlikely that any business will result as the competition will always have a better price for the customer. Spot dealing is not without its risks.

FORWARD DEALING

Chapter 2 discussed the relationship between spot and forward rates. Forward or futures dealing in foreign exchange is a foreign exchange deal for any date beyond the spot date. As mentioned, the foreign exchange can be bought or sold on an outright basis for a particular date at a particular rate, or it can be on a swap basis, which is when one currency is bought against another for one value date, either spot or forward, and then simultaneously sold against the same currency for another forward date.

Forward transactions are used by importers and exporters to protect themselves against a movement in the exchange markets and thereby in effect take out an insurance policy. Also, the forward markets can be used to protect a non-trade related exposure: for example, deals of a financial nature such as the protection of foreign currency capital if borrowed in one currency and used in another, or the placement of a loan or deposit in one currency which is different from the currency originally borrowed.

In Chapter 2, the following formula is proved:

$$\text{Forward Rate or Swap Differential} = \text{Spot Rate of Exchange} \times \frac{\text{No. of Days}}{360} \times \% \text{ p.a. Difference}$$

Since for most of the major currencies a forward market already exists, it is possible, using the above formula, to calculate the cost of the hedge as follows:

% p.a. Cost/Profit

$$= \frac{\text{Swap Differential} \times 360}{\text{Number of Days} \times \text{Spot Rate of Exchange} \times 100}$$

This is the basic interest arbitrage formula but it ignores the effect of the interest which would have to be paid or received if a borrowing and lending were to take place. It also does not allow for different methods of interest calculation, such as a year having 360 or 365 days. Therefore, an exporter or importer together with his bank can calculate the approximate cost in per cent per annum of executing a forward contract as a hedge to cover the risk. This can then be likened to the insurance premium.

It should also be realised that this percentage per annum might represent an extra profit to the exporter and not a cost. For example:

EXAMPLE 5.8

A UK exporter sells goods worth $1,000,000 in the USA.
Terms of trade: settlement in 180 days.
Spot rate of exchange: $/£ 1.9000–05
6 months' forward swap differential: 250–240 (a premium – so more expensive)
∴ Outright rates of exchange for 6 months = 1.8750–1.8765
∴ If the exporter today executes a forward contract with the bank whereby the $1,000,000 is sold to the bank for delivery in 6 months' time, the deal will be at the bank's buying rate of 1.8765. This will produce sterling to the exporter of £532,907. If a spot deal is done in 6 months time, the rate could be higher, lower, or the same as today at 1.9005. If the same, then $1,000,000 would produce £526,177 at 1.9005. Therefore, the exporter realises an additional profit of £6730 or 2.5 % p.a.

In some cases, dealing in the forward market and creating such a profit is then used by the exporter to reduce the price of the product in order to enable the exporter to be more competitive and thus ensure that the contract is won.

Using Example 5.8, had an importer been involved and had the importer wished to cover the foreign exchange exposure because a devaluation of the local currency was a real prospect, then the £6730 would not be a profit but an additional cost of 2.5 per cent p.a. Therefore:

1. When selling the forward foreign currency with the forward differential as a premium, a profit is made.
2. When buying the forward foreign currency with the forward differential as a premium, a loss is made. This is called a 'cost'.

If the foreign currency is at a discount (cheaper) forward, the converse of 1 and 2 would be true.

As all spot currencies are quoted against the US dollar then so are the forward currencies. However, using the same method as for calculating a spot cross rate of exchange, a forward outright rate can be established. For example:

EXAMPLE 5.9

Spot $/£	1.9000	Spot $/DM	2.1000
3 months forward differential	100 premium	3 months forward differential	200 premium
∴ Outright 3 months $/£	1.8900	∴ Outright 3 months $/DM	2.0800

∴ 3 months outright £/DM
$$= 1.8900 \times 2.0800$$
$$= 3.9312$$

and to express this as a swap, the spot £/DM
$$= 1.900 \times 2.1000$$
$$= 3.9900$$

∴ if the 3 months outright is subtracted –
$$-3.9312$$

the forward differential is
$$0.0588 \text{ premium}$$
or
$$5.9 \quad \% \text{ p.a.}$$

OUTRIGHT POSITIONS—HOW A BANK COVERS THE POSITION

So far the transactions have been considered from the customer's view. It is now necessary to see how the bank's dealing department would handle an outright foreign exchange forward transaction. Let us assume:

> The market for spot $/DM : 2.0000–2.0005
> Swap for 3 months $/DM : 200–190
> Swap for 6 months $/DM : 390–380

The bank's customer wishes to buy forward Deutschmarks against the sale of $1,000,000 for settlement in six months' time. The bank would have made the above quotes initially not knowing if the customer is a buyer or seller and would have been prepared to deal either way. Therefore:

Deal Bank sells forward Deutschmarks and buys US$1,000,000 for settlement in six months' time at *their* rate of exchange, 1.9610 $/DM (2.0000–390). Bank's foreign exchange position after this deal is +(long) $1,000,000 and—(short) DM1,961,000. But the bank's cash position does not reflect this until six months from now, when it will receive into its nostro account $1,000,000 and pay away to the customer DM1,961,000.

First Solution Do nothing until the value date becomes a spot date and then do a spot deal in the market whereby $1,000,000 is sold at the then spot rate and the equivalent amount of Deutschmarks is purchased. This is not recommended as it leaves the bank with a position for six months and an uncertain profit or loss.

Second Solution Try and find a bank with a position for the same value date but where they wish to buy US dollars and to sell Deutschmarks. If this can be done and the bank's dealer obtains an outright price of 1.9615–25 $/DM for six months' delivery, then the position opened by the original deal can be closed by the bank selling $1,000,000 for value six months at 1.9615 and in exchange receiving DM1,961,500.

	$	DM
Bank's foreign exchange position from original deal	+ 1,000,000	– 1,961,000
Bank's foreign exchange position after second solution	– 1,000,000	+ 1,961,500
	0	+ 500
		profit

Not only is the bank's dealing position cleared, so also is the cash position for the settlement day in six months' time. This is then an ideal solution; but supposing, whilst trying to cover, the market price had changed from the original deal price of 1.9610–1.9625 (the spot rates less the differentials) to 1.9595–1.9605? To cover in the above manner would now realise a loss since the sale

of $1,000,000 in cover would, at 1.9595, only produce
DM1,959,500, not DM1,961,000.
Third Solution Use the money market. Immediately the outright
six months' deal is done with a customer, the bank could execute
a spot foreign exchange contract.

	$	DM
Bank's foreign exchange position from original deal	+ 1,000,000	− 1,961,000
Bank's foreign exchange position after third solution	− 1,000,000	+ 2,000,000
	0	+ 39,000

Whilst the bank's dealer position in foreign exchange is covered,
a timing difference occurs with the cash in so far as DM2,000,000
will be received into the bank account in Germany which are not
needed for six months, whilst in the US$ nostro account an
overdraft will occur as $1,000,000 will be paid away and the cover
will not be received for six months. To resolve this, the
Deutschmarks could be invested for six months and $1,000,000
borrowed in the money market for six months. The profit to the
bank would then be as follows:

Profit on foreign exchange deal (difference between spot
and forward rates of exchange)   +
Income on investment of Deutschmarks for six months +
Loss on interest paid for borrowing dollars for six months −

Provided the first two pluses are greater than the minus, an
overall profit to the bank will occur.
Fourth Solution Use the swap foreign exchange market. This
may be necessary if the money market solution is impracticable –
if, for instance, no money market exists in the currencies
concerned or if the bank does not wish to use its balance sheet in
this manner. As in the third solution, a spot foreign exchange deal
would be completed in order to cover the dealer's foreign
exchange position but the cash timing difference would still be
there. By doing the reverse transaction in the foreign exchange
market, the dealer has created a 'swap' position. The advantage
to the trader is that a less risky situation has been created since
swap prices are generally less volatile than spot prices and the

original outright forward contract price was based on a particular spot rate of exchange.

	Cash a/c $		Cash a/c DM	
	DR	CR	DR	CR
Spot deal now		− 1,000,000	+ 2,000,000	
Original deal 6 months	+ 1,000,000			− 1,961,000

If another swap deal is now sought by the bank's trader whereby it is possible to do the reverse of the above at a different differential, a profit can be achieved as:

Original differential for 6 months	390–380
Current differential for 6 months	350–340
Spot rate now	1.9990–95

Therefore, to buy $1,000,000 spot and sell Deutschmarks, the dealer should deal at the other bank's selling rate of 1.9990. *Simultaneously*, the dealer sells the US$1,000,000 for six months' delivery and buys Deutschmarks for the same date. The other bank wishes to trade at the best rate to themselves since in this case they are the market, so a differential of 350 is used. Therefore, the forward rate is 1.9990−0.0350 = 1.9640. The cash accounts after this second swap deal now appear:

	Cash a/c $		Cash a/c DM	
	DR	CR	DR	CR
Spot deal now		− 1,000,000	+ 2,000,000	
Swap deal now	+ 1,000,000			− 1,999,000
Original deal 6 months	+ 1,000,000			− 1,961,000
Swap deal 6 months		− 1,000,000	+ 1,964,000	
Cash Position in 6 months	+ 2,000,000	− 2,000,000	+ 3,964,000	− 3,960,000

On this transaction, by 'swapping' the bank's dealing department has made a profit of DM4,000 (DM3,964,000–3,960,000). It is very important to realise that it is the swap differentials which matter, *not* the actual exchange rates, as shown below:

Original deal (spot deal and outright customer deal) differential	$= 2.0000 - 1.9610$
	$= .0390$
Swap deal (new spot deal and simultaneous forward) differential	$= 1.9990 - 1.9640$
	$= .0350$
Difference between the two differentials	$= .0390 - .0350$
	$= .0040$

∴ Profit = Original contract amount multiplied by difference
        between differentials
$$= \$1,000,000 \times DM.0040$$
$$= DM4000$$

N.B. Such forwards are quoted without the decimal point as
    390–350 for convenience.

This is the essence of swap or forward trading. It is the
differentials, not the actual rates of exchange, which must always
be considered.

As can be seen from the foregoing, the dealing department has
four solutions to the original customer deal. The one chosen will
depend upon which will produce the greatest profit.

FORWARD/FORWARD POSITION OR MISMATCH

In previous examples, the position has always been covered
exactly by the dealing department. In reality, a mismatch
situation could occur. During a working day many swaps will be
entered into, and at the end of the day the dealer's position in
foreign exchange could show zero but there could be some
settlement differences—'mismatches'. For example:

EXAMPLE 5.10 Cash flow in currencies

	Currency $	Currency DM
Spot	–	–
3 months	– 250,000	+ 495,000
6 months	+1,000,000	– 1,961,000
1 year	– 750,000	+ 1,447,500
Dealer's uncovered foreign exchange position	NIL	– 18,500

At the time the transactions were made, the forward premiums on the Deutschmarks were:

$$
\begin{array}{ll}
3 \text{ months} & -200- \\
6 \text{ months} & -390- \\
1 \text{ year} & -700-
\end{array}
$$

To close out these maturity 'gaps' a dealer may wish to:
1. Execute new swaps for spot against the appropriate forward date but the other way around.
2. Lend and borrow as previously shown.
3. Deal with a professional trader on a forward/forward basis.
In the above, this would necessitate dealing for three months against six months and/or six months against one year since this would cover the gaps.

The dealer's stand-in price for three months against six months is $390 - 200 = 190$ since it has already been established that in forward trading it is the differentials which matter, not the actual prices or rates. For six months against one year, the price is $700 - 390 = 310$. If the bank's dealing room can find other traders who will make forward quotations of (a) three months against six months and (b) six months against one year, it may be possible to close the gaps. If a price of $250 - 220$ is received for three months against six months, this would give a loss of 60 points $(250 - 190)$ as the margin is not in the favour of the position. If, on the other hand, a price of $390 - 70$ was quoted for six months against one year, the position could be closed at a profit of 60 points $(370 - 310)$.

If the dealing department was unhappy to retain these mismatches then the whole could be closed at a profit since, on closing three against six months, there is a loss of 60 points on $250,000 or DM1,500, but on six months against one year, there is a profit of 60 points on $750,000 or DM4,500. Therefore, on the deal there is a net profit of DM3,000.

Such forward/forward mismatches as in Example 5.10 occur in all dealing departments and are used as the basis for quoting to obtain business since the aim is to try to keep covering the gaps at profits.

It should be noted that gaps of just one day or overnight can occur since again this gives rise to a mismatch of settlement days. Again, to cover this, the swap technique or money market technique could both perhaps be considered.

OPTION CONTRACTS

Importers/exporters often wish to hedge their foreign exchange exposure with a forward contract but are uncertain as to which value date to choose as payment may be based on the day a ship docks or the day Bills of Lading are presented. To overcome this problem, option contracts are possible. This is a forward contract entered into by the importer/exporter with the bank where the importer/exporter has the right to take up the contract between two agreed dates. In exchange for giving the importer/exporter this option, the bank would normally make the price of the contract a little more expensive than a forward for a specific value date. For example:

EXAMPLE 5.11

Importer/exporter wishes to buy US$1,000,000 option two–three months from now and to sell pounds. Bank's dealing prices:

Spot	$/£ 1.9500–05
2 months	100–95 P
3 months	150–140 P

The option to buy dollars can be exercised by the customer up to the end of three months, so he would be quoted 1.9350 (1.9500 − 150) by the bank. This is the best possible price which the bank can offer to cover their exposure to deliver the money which could last until the end of the third month. Had the customer wished to sell US$1,000,000, then using the above rates for option second—third months, the bank would have quoted 1.9410 (1.9505 − 95) since this is the most favourable rate for the bank on the assumption that the customer sells at the earliest date. Therefore, if the customer actually settles on any other day, which is more than likely, then the original price was not the best which could have been obtained.

SPECULATION

As already mentioned, care must be taken in using the term 'speculation' which can mean anticipation, prudence or real speculation. Undoubtedly, speculation does occur and the forward market is a useful way of speculating. If it is felt that a currency will revalue or devalue in a reasonable period of time then an outright position is a way of making a profit on the change. However, if no change takes place, a loss could just as easily occur.

To create a speculative position, the weak currency is sold for future outright delivery and a strong currency is bought in exchange. As the volume of such orders increases, the forward differential can move away from the interest differential between the two centres, in which case interest arbitrage will occur. The forward differential will increase (widen) and the spot will weaken. This being so, a swap contract or a forward mismatch can also be created whilst the forward differential is still in line with the interest differential. In such a case, the weak currency should be purchased for the near date and sold for the far date against the stronger currency. Since interest rates of the weaker currency will normally rise and those of the stronger currency fall, a dealing department should ensure that it has covered any shortfalls in the cash position of the weak currency and at the same time that it is fully invested in the strong currency. It has been known for rates of 100–200 per cent p.a. to have been paid by speculators trying to finance their short positions and, on the other hand, for investors to have obtained zero or negative rates of interest for strong currencies on reinvestment.

The above is the textbook method of a dealing department establishing a bear position against a currency.

An alternative to creating the forward outright speculative position is the creation of a spot uncovered position. For example:

EXAMPLE 5.12

Spot $/DM: 2.0000–2.0025
Eurodollar deposit 1 month: $8\frac{1}{4}$–$8\frac{1}{2}$% p.a.
Euro-Deutschmark deposit 1 month: 3–$3\frac{1}{4}$% p.a.

Dealer decides to buy Deutschmarks and to sell dollars in

expectation of an appreciation in the rate of exchange for $/DM.

Deal A: At $/DM 2.0000, dealer sells $1,000,000 and buys DM2,000,000 value spot.

Deal B: Since dealer does not hold any of the dollars which have been sold in Deal A, he must borrow $1,000,000 for 1 month at $8\frac{1}{2}\%$ p.a.

Deal C: DM2,000,000 purchased in spot deal can be placed on deposit for 1 month at 3% p.a.

Deal D: At the end of one month $/DM is 1.9000 so dealer closes position by selling DM2,000,000 and buys dollar equivalent at this rate. As a result, dollar borrowing is repaid.

To calculate profit on transaction:

Deal A	DM2,000,000 purchased	$1,000,000	sold
Deal D	DM2,000,000 sold	$1,052,631	bought
	Difference	+$ 52,631	

Less Deal B. Cost of interest on borrowing dollars for 1 month at $8\frac{1}{2}\%$ p.a. $-$ 7,083

+$ 45,548

Plus Deal C. Interest income from DM deposit for 1 month at 3% p.a. is DM5,000 so dollar equivalent   +$ 2,631

Profit on Position   +$ 48,179

Whilst Example 5.12 gives a very satisfactory result, it should be noted that the borrowing had been arranged at the outset. If, however, the borrowing had been left and the market was so short of dollars that the rate of interest for overnight dollars rose to 100 per cent p.a., then each day's borrowing would cost $2.777 so the exchange rate would have to move significantly each day to compensate.

Currency speculation is something which can, and often does, backfire in that the currency does not change its parity, or a central bank intervenes with a bear squeeze, so great care is needed in the timing of taking such a position.

LIMIT ORDERS

In just the same manner as a commodity futures market, some dealing departments will receive and execute limit orders or 'at best' orders. Some will also leave such orders with brokers, other dealers or branches as a protection should something occur in another time-zone.

FORWARD VALUE DATES

All forward value dates are determined by reference to the spot value date which, as already discussed, is two business days from the contract date. A forward value date is then one calendar month, or two, or three, etc., from the spot date, provided that the end date is also a business day in both centres. If the calendar period is a weekend or a public holiday then the forward value date is the next business day. The only time this does not apply is when the spot date falls on the last working day of the month or when the spot date falls on a date which is numerically in excess of the last working day of a future month. In such cases, month-end to month-end is used.

BROKERS

In all the examples, banks have been shown as dealing directly with other banks or dealing with a customer. In practice, a large percentage of the bank to bank dealing is undertaken through brokers. Why?

Brokers are in contact with large numbers of banks and act as intermediaries. They normally do not take positions in a currency but in certain centres this is not the case. A broker provides a bank's dealing department with a service in exchange for which a small fee is paid as a fixed percentage of the value of the deal. The amount paid varies from centre to centre, from currency to currency, and depends upon the type of deal, e.g. spot, forward or deposit.

The broker is in contact with large numbers of banks on a very regular basis and, therefore, is often able to put buyer and seller, lender and borrower together at better prices than the bank bid and offer prices. This is possible in that by working with so many banks, a broker has many prices from which to choose and can, therefore, select the best price to suit a particular bank's requirements. Brokers quote a bank a price—normally bid and asked. If a bank wishes to deal, an indication must be given by the bank of the amount and whether a buyer or seller. The broker will then try to bring the two parties together. However, it should be noted that whilst price and amount may be acceptable, the counterparties may not be acceptable to each other. Therefore, part of a broker's skill lies not just in quoting a price but also in knowing who can deal with whom, i.e. the broker must be aware of an individual bank's policy with regard to inter-bank foreign exchange and placement limits.

Close competitive prices are usually found in spot trading or in forward trading up to six months' value date since this is where most of the activity occurs in the markets. As the period lengthens and there are fewer counterparties, so the quotations will widen as there are not so many buyers and sellers. To compensate for this, the price is widened in order to entice a dealer with the prospect of the extra profit obtainable through the wider difference between bid and asked. It is possible, in the major currencies, to deal for up to five years in the future but the difference between bid and asked is wide.

PART B. DEPOSITS

Deposit dealings are as much a part of the dealing function as foreign exchange since the two are so closely interrelated. As with foreign exchange dealing, quotations are given by a dealer as bid and asked, e.g. $7-7\frac{1}{4}$ per cent p.a. This means that a rate of 7 per cent p.a. will be paid for a deposit and a rate of $7\frac{1}{4}$ per cent p.a. charged to a borrower.

SOURCES OF FUNDS

Banks receive deposits from numerous sources: customers; other banks; central banks; governments; international organisations;

pension funds, etc. Most deposits are clean or unsecured but some will have been obtained by issuing a Certificate of Deposit or some other negotiable instruments such as a floating rate note, a bond, etc.

Whilst a large proportion, usually between one third and one half of a commercial bank's deposits, are interest-free since they represent a customer's working balance, the remainder is usually bought money—in other words, deposits against which a bank will have to pay interest. Such deposits will either be in the local currency of the bank or branch or will be Euro-deposits. The Euro-market grew during the 1960s and 1970s to a current size of in excess of $600 billion. Of this, something between 75 and 80 per cent is in the form of Eurodollar deposits. The problem is that much of this sum is in interest-bearing time deposits with an average life of less than three months.

USE OF FUNDS

Given the size of the market and the short maturities of the Euro-market deposits, how are they used? The preservation of a bank's liquidity is very important and so lending long and borrowing short is dangerous. None the less, the funds must be used, must be used profitably, must preserve liquidity and must fund commercial loans.

LIQUIDITY

Consider the following two banks:

	($ million) Bank A				($ million) Bank B		
Deposits	1000	Loans	200	Deposits	1000	Loans	800
		Redeposits	800			Redeposits	200
	1000		1000		1000		1000

Bank A is said to be more liquid than Bank B since it could lose nearly $800 million of its redeposits (inter-bank time deposits with other banks) before it would have to be concerned as to whether it could continue to fund its loan portfolio, whereas Bank B could only lose $200 million of redeposits. Therefore, part of the reason for inter-bank redeposit dealing is to provide liquidity for the bank, it being assumed that such inter-bank placements are with counterparties of the highest integrity and the maturities compare favourably with the maturity structure of the deposit portfolio.

PROFITABILITY

Profitability will come from one of three sources:

1. Float, which is the use of interest-free funds;
2. Spread, which is the difference between rates paid for a deposit and the rates earned and
3. Mismatch, which is a timing difference to create a deposit gap or an exchange exposure.

1. *Float* This refers to money available to a dealing department before it is required to meet a scheduled payment. To be more exact, this can be called 'positive float', 'negative float' being the reverse, when funds are paid away before they have been received. For example:

EXAMPLE 5.13

Customer sells $1,000,000 to a bank for value spot against purchase of Deutschmarks. Instead of paying by telegraphic transfer on the spot date, the customer on the contract date gives the bank a cheque for $1,000,000 drawn on New York. If the bank is able to clear the cheque and obtain good funds tomorrow then positive float is created for one day. As a result, the bank can invest $1,000,000 in the overnight deposit market at the prevailing rate of interest.

2. *Spread*

EXAMPLE 5.14

Bank borrows $1,000,000 from a customer for six months at 7% p.a. and lends to another counterparty for six months at $7\frac{1}{2}\%$ p.a. The bank makes a spread of $\frac{1}{2}\%$ p.a. As shown in Chapter 3, it may be possible for the spread to be increased by the forward sale of the interest.

3. *Mismatch* If it is anticipated that interest rates are going to decline then to lend long and borrow short should produce a profit. If, on the other hand, it is anticipated that interest rates will rise then to borrow long and to lend short should produce a profit. The second alternative is much sounder banking than the first since the bank is more liquid. However, due to the very nature of its business, the bank normally finds itself in the first situation.

Example of a dealer's mismatch:

EXAMPLE 5.15

$1,000,000 deposit placed for 30 days at 8% p.a.
$1,000,000 deposit taken for 7 days at 7% p.a.

Dealers therefore have a funding gap in so far as in seven days time a new deposit must be taken for 23 days or some shorter period as the deposit placed will not be repaid for 30 days. If nothing is done, an overdraft will occur.

To calculate the rate which can be paid for the final 23 days:

Method 1

Earning 30 days at 8% p.a. $= 30 \times 8 = 240$
Less paying 7 days at 7% p.a. $= 7 \times 7 = 49$
Period left 23 days at X% p.a. $= 23 \times X = 191$
$$X\% \text{ p.a.} = 8.3\%$$
∴ A rate of 8.3% p.a. could be paid for the remaining 23 days in which case there would be no profit or loss. If a lower rate is paid, a profit on the whole transaction will result—if higher, a loss.

This method, whilst simple, is only a guide because at the end of seven days it is not just the principal of $1,000,000 which must be borrowed but also the interest of $1361.11, being 7% on $1,000,000 for seven days. Therefore, it is the following which must be used in practice:

Method 2

Period A = number of days from start to first maturity.
Period B = number of days from first forward maturity to final maturity.

Period C = total number of days from start to final (total number of days).

Funding Cost % p.a. of interest

$$= \frac{\text{Period A} \times \text{Rate for Period A} \times \text{Period B} \times \text{Rate for Period B}}{\text{Period C} \times 360 \times 100}$$

Using above in the example:

$$\text{Funding Cost \% p.a.} = \frac{7 \times 7 \times 23 \times 8}{30 \times 360 \times 100}$$
$$= .008\%$$

To take this funding cost into the calculation of the forward/forward price, it is necessary to multiply by the total number of days and divide by the Period B. So, in our example, effect of funding interest is $.010\% \left(\frac{.008 \times 30}{23} \right)$

∴ Method 1 gave a rate of 8.3% p.a.
Actual rate to be used is 8.3% − .010% = 8.29%.

The longer the period and the higher the rates of interest the more important is this interest factor. Watching the timing of receipt and payment of interest can change the yield on a deposit significantly. Also, whilst normal Euro-market practice is exact number of days on a 360-day year basis, some deposit markets, such as sterling, use a 365-day year. Therefore, if it is necessary to compare interest rates, an adjustment should always be made by taking the sterling rate of interest and multiplying by 365 and dividing by 360.

Another type of mismatch can occur between currencies. This will result in an uncovered foreign exchange position and a possible matching in the deposit position. For example:

EXAMPLE 5.16

> Borrow Swiss francs 1,000,000 for 30 days at 1%
> Sell the Swiss francs for spot settlement against a purchase of US dollars at a rate of exchange of $/SFcs 2.
> Lend the resultant $500,000 for 30 days at 10%
> Apparent profit: 9%

In 30 days time, Swiss franc deposit will have to be repaid. One solution is to buy the Swiss francs by selling the US dollars from the maturing deposit. If the rate of exchange is the same then, indeed, a profit of 9 % is made. A lucky profit! If, however, the rate of exchange is now 1.85 $/SFcs then the following will result:

Interest paid on borrowing	= SFcs 833	(−)
Interest earned on loan	= $4,166	(+)
Loss on exchange		
SFcs 1,000,000 at 2 = $500,000		
1,000,000 at 1.85 = $540,540	= $40,540	(−)

Plus $4,166, minus $40,540, minus $450 (equivalent of SFcs 833) means a total loss of $36,824. This is obviously not a satisfactory outcome for the dealing department. Such an operation should only be undertaken with care in the near certainty of which way an exchange rate will move. At the outset of such a transaction, the break-even exchange rate should be calculated and evaluated to see if it is a realistic and acceptable risk:

Formula:

$$\text{Break-even Rate} = \text{Current Spot Rate} - \left(\text{Current Spot Rate} \times \text{Annualised Interest Differential} \times \frac{\text{No. of days}}{360} \right)$$

INTEREST ARBITRAGE

This may be defined as the conversion of a deposit received in one currency into a deposit in another currency on a fully hedged basis.

Figure 5.1 shows the ingredients of an interest arbitrage transaction. Such deals are used by banks, companies and other investors when they wish to make a loan, provide capital, purchase a security, etc., but are not willing to accept an uncovered risk. The constituent parts are always:

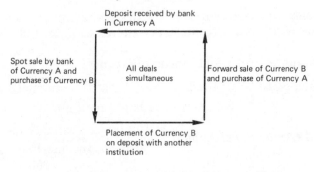

FIG. 5.1 Diagram of a covered deposit interest arbitrage

(a)	Cost of borrowing	minus	known at outset
(b)	Income on loan	plus	known at outset
(c)	Profit/cost on difference between spot and forward exchange rates—swap differential.	plus/minus	$\dfrac{\text{Premium/Discount} \times 360 \times 100}{\text{No. of days} \times \text{spot rate of exchange}}$

If the deal is to be attractive then the sum of (a) + (b) + (c) should show a profit. If a profit cannot be obtained and if there are no other considerations such as balance-sheet capital ratios, then it would be better to make the loan and to borrow the funds in the same currency to minimise the exchange risk.

The above, however, does not take into account the actual payment and receipt of interest. The interest will be received in one currency and paid away in another. If the currency in which the interest is to be received weakens then at the maturity of the deal it may not realise, upon conversion at the spot rate then prevailing, sufficient to pay the interest due. There is, therefore, a foreign exchange risk or position in the interest to be paid and received. To eliminate this, the interest should be covered on a forward basis at the time that the original deal is consummated and the cost or profit used in determining the true result of the whole transaction. This can be done by a separate forward deal or by inclusion in the original foreign exchange swap transaction. Whichever method is used, the additional income or expense resulting from the hedge must then be either added to or deducted from the original income or expense of the swap transaction. This additional consideration can be expressed as an amount as in formula (a) or as a percentage per annum as in formula (b):

(a) Amount of Additional Income/Expense

$$= \frac{\text{Interest to be received/paid} \times \text{Forward Premium/Discount}}{\text{Base Currency Exchange Rate}}$$

(b) Percentage Per Annum $= \dfrac{\text{Additional Income/Expense}}{\text{Original Income/Expense}}$

$$\times\, 100 \times \frac{360}{\text{No. of days}}$$

Therefore, to calculate the true swap income/expense as a percentage per annum, the basic swap interest differential formula and the interest hedge must be added together. When combined this produces:

(c) % p.a. cost/profit with the interest covered

$$= \frac{\left(\dfrac{360}{\text{No. of days}} + \dfrac{\text{Base Currency Euro-deposit Rate}}{100} \right)}{\text{Spot Rate of Exchange} \times 100}$$
$$\times \text{Forward Premium/Discount}$$

Definitions

'Base currency' is the currency which, when multiplied by the exchange rate, produces the principal currency, e.g.

$$\$/DM = \$1 \times 2.00 = DM2 \qquad \text{Base currency dollars}$$
$$\$/\pounds = \pounds 1 \times 1.95 = \$1.95 \qquad \text{Base currency pounds}$$

'Base currency Euro-deposit rate' is the rate of interest for the base currency for the relevant period.

The method used to calculate the percentage per annum cost with the interest covered forward is illustrated in Example 5.17.

EXAMPLE 5.17

6 months (181 days) dollar deposit rate
of interest $\qquad = 9\frac{5}{8}\%$ p.a.

6 months (181 days) Deutschmark
deposit rate of interest $\qquad = 4\%$ p.a.

Spot \$/DM = 1.9550

6 months swap \$/DM = 560

By using formula (c): % p.a. swap profit

$$= \frac{\left(\dfrac{360}{181} + \dfrac{9.625}{100}\right) 560}{1.9550 \times 100}$$

$$= 5.973\% \text{ p.a.}$$

∴ 6 months Deutschmarks can be created from dollars at 3.65% p.a. (9.625 − 5.973) which is cheaper than the market cost of Deutschmarks—hence a profit will be made on lending at 4% p.a.

Proof

\$1,000,000 borrowed for 181 days at $9\frac{5}{8}\%$ p.a. will cost \$48,392.36 in interest. Therefore, \$1,048,392.36 will be payable at maturity.

Swap: Spot sale of dollars against Deutschmarks \$1,000,000 at 1.9550 = DM1,955,000.00

Forward purchase of dollars against Deutschmarks including forward cover of interest \$1,048,392.36 at 1.8990 (1.9550 − .0560) = DM1,990,897.09

= DM 35,897.09

If this final amount is then annualised and expressed as a percentage of the original amount of Deutschmarks, it is equal to 3.65% p.a. which is the cost of creating the Deutschmarks from the formula.

As a corollary, this technique can be used to see how best funds can be invested. For example:

EXAMPLE 5.18

Solution A

Bank dealing department receives a deposit in Swiss francs for 3 months at 2% p.a.

> Lend Swiss francs for 3 months at $2\frac{1}{8}$% p.a.
> Profit: $\frac{1}{8}$% p.a.

Solution B:

> Lend US dollars for 3 months at +8% p.a.
> Swap cost covering interest
>   using above formula is   −5% p.a.
> Cost of borrowing Swiss francs −2% p.a.
> _____
> +1% p.a.

∴ It is better to make a swap as profit is more attractive.

Situations such as in Example 5.18 are encountered regularly in a treasury department. Therefore, it is useful to understand the method used in order to be able to maximise profits.

INTER-CENTRE ARBITRAGE

Because of such excellent world-wide communication systems, it is rare for a dealer to be able to borrow in one centre and to simultaneously lend in another for the same period and to show a profit unless the credit risk is dissimilar. Therefore, whilst in theory it is possible, it usually only occurs if markets are very hectic.

ROLL-OVER CREDITS

Many medium-term loans are financed with Eurocurrencies on a roll-over basis. To overcome one of the basic problems of the Euro-market, i.e. an excess supply of short-term deposits and a demand for longer-term credits, the roll-over concept was developed. A bank enters into a medium-term commitment as to maturity and amount but to protect its interest rate exposure it determines that the interest rate shall vary during the life of the loan. The Euro-market concept is, therefore, to lend on a cost-plus basis for a shorter period, i.e. a margin is added to whatever is the cost of financing to the bank for the appropriate period. The margin reflects the cost of capital, the cost of the risk and the cost of administration of the loan. Because the loan is for a medium term and the deposits which are obtainable are normally of a one, three or six-month maturity, it is necessary for the bank's dealers to fund the loan by borrowing for, say, six months and then, at the maturity of the deposit, borrow again for another period of six months; and so on. This is called rolling-over a loan. Every six months a new rate will be charged to the borrower representing the cost to the bank of obtaining the currency for the next six months plus the margin. The most used rate is LIBOR—The London Interbank Offered Rate—which is the rate at which prime banks could obtain funds in the London Euro-market. The dealing department must then include this roll-over in its own money position.

STAND-BY CREDITS

Because there is no lender of last resort in the Euro-markets, some foreign banks and their dealing departments have arranged back-up facilities from banks with a local currency base, i.e. American banks have sterling, Swiss franc and Deutschmark back-up facilities from English, Swiss and German banks; English banks have US dollars, Swiss franc, and Deutschmark back-up facilities from American, Swiss and German banks, etc. The idea is that in the event of a bank being unable to fund itself in its non-local currency, it has a lender of last resort.

Branches normally look to their head office for support. In the case of American banks, their head office, if a member of the Federal Reserve, can in an emergency call upon the Federal Reserve bank for support. Therefore, the US dollar market is perhaps not as exposed as originally thought, but with a Euro-market of over $600 billion it is doubtful, should a crisis come, if the amount of support would be forthcoming.

THURSDAY/FRIDAY AND WEEKEND US DOLLAR DEALING

The settlement method between banks in the United States causes a problem for the Eurodollar market.

Cheques drawn by customers of banks in the United States are cleared through the local clearing house of that particular Federal Reserve district. At the end of the day, the balances (debit or credit) are listed by the clearing house and a memorandum furnished to the particular Federal Reserve bank and the commercial member banks. The *following* day, settlement is made between the member banks using their accounts at the Federal Reserve banks. This settlement takes place the *same* day.

The foregoing gives rise to two types of fund in the United States—Clearing House Funds and Federal Funds. The former comprises balances of accounts maintained by customers with the member banks and the latter the balances of the member banks with the Federal Reserve. It is the Federal Funds which interest the member banks since they represent their actual available cash after deducting their Federal Reserve cash reserve requirements.

The majority of all foreign exchange and Eurodollar money market transactions are made in clearing funds since the settlement takes place between customers of the American banks. The clearing house used for the majority of Euro-transactions is that of New York. Thus, a Euro-transaction today becomes a Federal Funds transaction tomorrow. For example:

EXAMPLE 5.19

Euro-Bank A lends $1,000,000 to Euro Bank B from Tuesday to Wednesday:
Whilst in Example 5.19 the Euro-banks settle Tuesday/Wednesday, the New York correspondent banks settle Wednesday/Thursday. Because of this 'one day later' or 'following day' method of settlement, it follows that a Euro-deposit Thursday to Friday (one day) is a Federal Funds.Friday to Monday (three day) deposit and that a Euro-deposit Friday to Monday (three day) is a Federal Funds deposit Monday to Tuesday (one day).

If no adjustment were to be made to the Eurodollar deposit rates to reflect the above, arbitrage could occur. For example, an American bank, through its Euro-branch, could borrow US

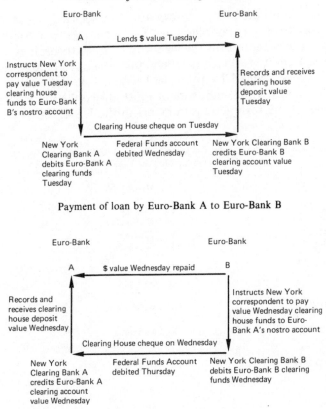

Payment of loan by Euro-Bank A to Euro-Bank B

Repayment of the loan by Euro-Bank B to Euro-Bank A

dollars in the Euro-market from Thursday to Friday and pay one day's interest, but would be able to invest the funds in the US Federal Funds Market for three days and hence receive three days' interest. Similarly, the bank would make a loan in the Euro-market for the weekend (three days) and cover by borrowing Federal Funds for one day Monday/Tuesday. Therefore, the Euro-deposit rates must be adjusted. If Thursday to Friday Federal Funds are 5 per cent p.a., Friday to Monday Federal Funds are 5 per cent p.a. and Monday to Tuesday Federal Funds are 5 per cent p.a., then Euro-rates for a normal day should also trade at or near 5 per cent p.a. after the adjustment for reserve requirements. Since it has been shown that a Euro-deposit Thursday/Friday is equal to three days Federal Funds, the Euro-rate is multiplied by three to compensate, such that Thursday/Friday Eurodollars will be 15 per cent p.a. Similarly, whilst a Euro-deposit for the weekend is worth three days, in the Federal Funds Market it is worth only one day. Therefore, the Euro-rate is divided by three to become 1.66 per cent p.a. It should be noted that adjustment must always be made in rates because of the reserve requirements in the USA.

Interest basis 5 % a day. (Total for week must equal 35 %. No. of days × rate per day = total for the week.)

Normal Week			Monday Shut	
Monday	5		Tuesday	5
Tuesday	5		Wednesday	5
Wednesday	5		Thursday	19
Thursday	14		W/E & Monday (4 × 1.5 %)	6
W/E (3 × 2 %)	6			35 %
	35 %			

Tuesday Shut			Wednesday Shut	
Monday & Tuesday (2 × 2.5 %)	5		Monday	10
Wednesday	5		Tuesday & Wednesday (2 × 2.5 %)	5
Thursday	14		Thursday	14
W/E (3 × 3.666 %)	11		W/E (3 × 2 %)	6
	35 %			35 %

Thursday Shut			Friday Shut	
Monday	5		Monday	5
Tuesday	10		Tuesday	5
Wednesday & Thursday (2 × 7 %)	14		Wednesday	19
W/E (3 × 2 %)	6		Thursday & W/E (4 × 1.5 %)	6
	35 %			35 %

FIG. 5.2 Interest obtained from holidays under the Federal Reserve System

This technical problem recurs in the Euro-market if, for example, a Monday is a holiday in the USA, as the above sums must be redone to reflect a four-day weekend, not a three-day weekend.

Care must be taken when trading Eurodollar deposits to always note what is the start day, what is the end day and if a holiday in the United States will affect either. If a deposit is made for a period which does not have the same number of Thursdays/Fridays and weekends to compensate each other, the deposit rate will be distorted—the shorter the period the greater the distortion, and the higher the interest rates the greater the distortion.

This technical feature of deposit dealing in Eurodollars also affects the exchange markets since swap rates are based on interest differentials and, therefore, as dollar rates of interest move for technical reasons, then so must swap rates against the US dollar.

As already shown, another way of obtaining a US dollar deposit is, instead of borrowing, to buy them against the uncovered sale of another currency and to borrow this other currency. No other Euro-centre has this one-day-later method of clearing, only the USA. For example:

EXAMPLE 5.20

1. Borrow Swiss francs Thursday/Friday at 1% p.a.
   Sell Swiss francs value Thursday and buy US dollars at, say, an exchange rate of $/SF 2.
   Lend resultant dollars at 15% p.a. Thursday to Friday.
   Apparent Profit : 14% p.a.
or 2. Lend sterling Friday/Monday at 10% p.a.
   Sell dollars to produce sterling at $/£ 1.90 value Friday.
   Borrow dollars from Friday to Monday at 2% p.a.
   Apparent Profit : 8% p.a.

The apparent profits in Example 5.20 will *only* occur if, upon reconverting, the spot exchange rate is unaltered. To compensate, the foreign exchange spot rates should move up or down by an amount equivalent to the swap cost or interest differential. Therefore, for value on a Friday currencies will usually look strong against the US dollar and weaker on Thursday and Mondays provided there is no other factor to be considered.

When comparing exchange rates or deposit rates, it is best to choose a neutral day, such as for value on a Wednesday, since otherwise the rate may be distorted as a result of the foregoing.

NEGOTIABLE INSTRUMENTS

Some dealing departments trade in such instruments as Certificates of Deposit, Bills of Exchange, Floating Rate Notes, etc. The principles of deposit dealing still apply but the dealer has greater flexibility since not only are they held for the running profit (difference between cost of money and yield on asset) but there is also the possibility of a capital profit by selling at a lower yield. Such instruments are very profitable in a falling rate market. Banks often prefer to hold such instruments for liquidity or because it enables them to trade using limited assets but obtain the same yield as a much larger bank. For example:

EXAMPLE 5.21

Bank A   Redeposits $10 million spread $\frac{1}{4}$% p.a.
             Income   : $25,000

Bank B   Redeposits $5 million spread $\frac{1}{4}$% p.a.
             Income   : $12,500
             Also buys Bills $5 million and
             Sells Bills $5 million on which a $\frac{1}{4}$% p.a.
                capital profit
             Income   : $12,500

Whilst both banks have the same income, the return on the assets of Bank B is higher.

Floating Rate Notes can also be interesting investments since, in times of low interest rates, the minimum coupon which is often included in the original terms and conditions can make these appear as very attractive investments to a dealing department. The ultimate maturity should be watched to ensure that they are really banking assets and not bond or long-term assets.

6 Dealing Risks

Dealing in the foreign exchange and deposit markets is not without its risks. History has shown that large sums can be lost as well as made in the money markets. Consequently, extreme care is needed in dealing. It is, therefore, necessary to discuss the various types of risk involved in order that they may be evaluated.

CREDIT RISK

All foreign exchange and money market transactions involve dealing with someone else. As a result, the quality of the counterparty is important since, unless sound, the counterparty will be unable to fulfil the obligation of either repaying the loan or deposit or settling the foreign exchange contract. Thus, all banks should, out of prudence, analyse the strength of their counterparties. This is often done by an annual or regular credit review of the counterparty. At the time of such a review, a limit is normally established as to how much business a bank feels it prudent to transact with a specific counterparty in both redeposits and foreign exchange. Such amounts are often established by reference to the size of the counterparty's capital, its gearing, profitability, management ability and country of location. For placements or redeposits, the amount granted usually varies between 10 and 25 per cent of capital and for foreign exchange transactions a multiple of this figure is used, often as high as ten.

The distinction between the two types of risk is important. If a placement is made with a counterparty who subsequently goes bankrupt, then the whole amount of the loan is lost. Banks fail as well as corporations and, therefore, it is not uncommon for redeposits to be placed at different rates for the same periods but with different counterparties since this rate differential reflects a higher risk. This is called a two-tier market.

With a foreign exchange transaction, there are two types of

77

risk. If a counterparty becomes bankrupt before the maturity of the deal or is for some reason unable to fulfil the obligations of the contract then the dealing department will not settle the contract on the due date. One must remember that a foreign exchange contract is an exchange of currencies on a given date—nothing happens until that day. If, therefore, settlement is unable to take place, the dealing department will cancel the outstanding contract and then re-enter the foreign exchange market and undertake a new deal for the same maturity date. The risk to the bank is the difference between the exchange rate on the original contract and the exchange rate on the new contract. This risk used to be evaluated at around 10 per cent of the nominal amount of the contract: now that markets are more volatile, a figure of 20–25 per cent might be more appropriate.

The second risk in a foreign exchange transaction occurs on the day of settlement. Because of different countries and different time-zones, one counterparty may have given instructions to pay its part of a foreign exchange deal before the cover has been received. If, in the middle of settlement, a bankruptcy occurs then the loss to the bank could be 100 per cent of the contract amount. As a precaution, many banks limit the amount of foreign exchange which can be settled with any one counterparty on a particular day to, say, 10 or 20 per cent of the total foreign exchange limit with some form of minimum amount.

Problems such as the above were highlighted by the failure of the Bankhaus I. D. Herstatt in June 1974. This bank was closed by the German authorities during the day because of large losses and both of the above types of credit risk became realities. Forward contracts were cancelled uncompleted. Contracts for settlement on the day the bank was closed were initially a 100 per cent loss to banks, but as the bankruptcy proceedings progressed this loss was reduced.

TRANSFER RISK

A transfer or country risk is a specialised type of credit risk. As long as lending and borrowing occurs between local banks in the local currency of the country, the transfer risk is not a matter of real concern. If, however, a foreign currency is lent by a non-resident of the country or by a resident, then the transfer risk must be considered. For example, if a country closes its foreign exchange markets, a counterparty cannot sell the local currency in order to purchase foreign currency to repay the debt, notwithstanding that they have the local funds necessary to effect repayment. Countries too exhaust their foreign currency reserves and whilst they can print more local money, always at a cost to themselves, they cannot print foreign currency. Therefore, defaults or delays in payment from countries like Zaire, North Korea, Egypt, Turkey and Peru have occurred.

Anyone operating in a country, regardless of the nationality of the shareholder, is, or could be, liable to the transfer risk problem.

OPERATIONAL RISK

Problems will occur if a counterparty has inefficient operating staff or pays through an inefficient correspondent. Whilst payment is eventually assured, assuming the credit risk to be satisfactory the inconvenience and trouble caused can often remove any profit on the deal. In such cases, banks will sometimes not pay in an exchange deal until confirmation has been received that the countervalue is held by their correspondents, or may not release a Certificate of Deposit until a similar confirmation is received. Margin accounts are also sometimes held for just such an eventuality. The bank normally looks to the counterparty to rectify any losses or expenses.

RATE RISK

Any time a bank's dealing department has a mismatch in its deposit and redeposit portfolio or its forward exchange operations, or is over-bought or over-sold in its foreign exchange position, it has a rate risk. For example:

EXAMPLE 6.1

A bank has borrowed six months' money in expectation of rates increasing and has paid 9 % p.a. for them. For the first month it lends the funds in the market at $8\frac{3}{4}$ % p.a., accepting the negative spread since it is sure of making it up over the final five months. However, if, instead of going up the rates decrease to 7 % because of an influx of foreign money, the bank faces a loss of $\frac{1}{4}$ % p.a. for month one and 2 % p.a. for months two to six. This equates to an actual loss of $18,750 per one million dollars or for just a $10 million position, a loss of $187,500! Therefore, whilst the bank had been prudent in borrowing long and lending short, it had none the less encountered a severe loss.

If long of a deposit, the most a bank can normally lose is the difference between the rate paid for the deposit and leaving the funds idle, earning no interest, in a correspondent nostro account. The word 'normally' is used since in some countries, e.g. Switzerland, Germany and Japan, regulations have been introduced limiting the amounts which can be held without a penalty being paid. In such cases it is often better to lend at a negative rate of interest just to remove the funds from the account.

If a bank has over-lent or is short in deposits then there is no limit to the rate which might have to be paid to cover the position. In such circumstances, it must pay the rate or go bankrupt. Such rates can be high—in 1967 for Eurosterling it was 1000 per cent p.a. for overnight funds, and in 1972 for Eurodollars 40 per cent p.a. for overnight funds.

A foreign exchange rate risk occurs if there is an uncovered over-bought or over-sold position. For example:

EXAMPLE 6.2

Dealer Foreign Exchange Position:

Plus $1,000,000   Short DM2,000,000
Stand-in rate: $/DM 2.0000

If the Deutschmark appreciates in value or the US dollar depreciates, the rate of exchange will move against this position. Each one pfennig move or 100 points will cost the bank DM10,000 or $5000. Therefore, all uncovered positions or uncovered balances must be either a part of a deliberate policy to hold such a position or should be covered since it could otherwise prove expensive.

Another type of risk occurs if a bank holds a swap position. For example:

EXAMPLE 6.3

	$	£
3 months forward	+ 1,000,000	− 500,000
6 months forward	− 1,000,000	+ 502,512 Swap Differential + 100 points

Nil uncovered foreign exchange position $ and £.

The view has been taken in Example 6.3 that the swap differential will decrease because the interest rate differential between the two currencies will decrease since, for example, it is expected that whilst US dollar interest rates will remain steady, sterling interest rates will fall. The covering of this position can occur in one of two ways—by another swap (the foreign exchange method) or by a loan and deposit (the money market method).

When the view of falling interest rates in sterling was taken by lending pounds long and borrowing short, the rate risk only concerned one currency. In Example 6.3, two currencies are involved. Therefore, whilst sterling rates may indeed fall, should US dollars also fall the interest differential may not change, so the swap may not change. Alternatively, domestic sterling rates may fall but Eurosterling, upon which the swap rate is based, may hold because of the expected weakness of the currency. In other words, for a swap exposure there are always two variables to consider.

LIQUIDITY RISK

If a placement or redeposit position is over-lent, or if, because of a swap, there is an imbalance in a cash flow, there is a risk of not being able to obtain funds to cover the cash deficit. Provided that the bank's credit is still good, money can usually be obtained for any period, no matter how tight the market, but a price will have to be paid. However, the liquidity risk cannot be ignored since markets can close, can become one-way (all sellers and no buyers) and central banks can impose controls.

FRAUD

Fraud is a risk which can occur in any business. If it occurs in money dealing, the losses involved can be large—Banque de

Bruxelles, Lloyds Bank Lugano, Gotabanken and Franklin National Bank are all examples. Therefore, control procedures (limits, audits) are all-important. However, if there is collusion amongst staff, be it between dealer and operations department or management and dealer, there is little that can be done to stop the fraud being perpetrated. It is, therefore, imperative that dealers be well supervised, honest and well trained and that systems be in place to try and prevent such an occurrence.

The reasons for the perpetration of frauds have varied in so far as in certain cases there has been no personal gain to the individual dealer. For example, the wrong position may have been created and the dealer was unwilling to admit the mistake and he chose to hide it in the belief that the position would come right some time. Other frauds have, none the less, occurred for personal gain. A dealer may have decided to deal for his own account and make a profit at the expense of a bank or he may have been in receipt of a bribe in exchange for executing a particular transaction.

Fortunately, frauds are rare but when discovered the losses involved are large.

EXCHANGE CONTROL RISK

Some countries impose tight exchange control restrictions on the movement of funds between countries. Therefore, it is essential that dealers be trained and understand the rules, and systems be in place to ensure that compliance with local exchange control is adhered to at all times. The risk is that if it is discovered by the local authorities that a bank has broken an exchange control regulation, the bank will be fined and/or lose its licence to operate and the dealer will lose his job, be fined and/or go to jail.

In conclusion, there are risks involved, but they can be evaluated as to their likelihood. Of all those discussed, the rate risk is the one with which most banks' dealing rooms have to contend. However, all the others are always present and must be considered.

7 Management of the Foreign Exchange and Deposit Dealing Functions

Because of the importance of the role of foreign exchange and money market activities to an international bank, it is imperative that such activities be properly controlled and managed. Not only do the dealing department and the individual dealers need to know their positions or exposures in a particular currency but so does management since, if they are not known, the correct decision on trading policy cannot be made.

REPORTING OF POSITIONS

Whilst every bank will use as a format for a report one which suits its own individual requirements, it is none the less essential that the following types of report be produced on a regular basis which, for large banks, should mean daily.

The first type of report should consider what is the dealer's total uncovered over-bought or over-sold position in any one currency against the local currency. Such a record is maintained by the position clerk in both the dealing department and in the operations department but as a control and verification it should also be independently produced and checked by the accounting department. Such a report might appear as Figure 7.1.

Whilst a foreign exchange position might originally have been 'sold US dollars bought Swiss francs', it is doubtful if, at the end of a trading day, the amounts would exactly equal each other at the closing spot rate of exchange for the day. Any difference must, therefore, be a position against either another currency or the local currency. In order to simplify this, if all positions are compared to the local currency, a total net position of all currencies can be obtained. Not only is such a report essential to

Foreign Currency Position Report as at . . .			
Closing Spot Rate	Over-bought/Over-sold		Local Currency
	+	−	Equivalent
US dollars			
Swiss francs			
Deutschmarks			
Yen			
French francs			
Guilders			
[etc.]			
Total Net Foreign Exchange Position +/−			

FIG. 7.1 Sample foreign currency position report

the bank, but the position must also be monitored daily since in certain countries central banks place limits on local banks, branches or affiliates of foreign banks as to how much is permitted to be held as a net foreign exchange position of all currencies over-bought or over-sold for whatever period against the local currency. This is to control speculation in the local currency. A report such as Figure 7.1 should also be produced regularly by any dealing department of any branch or overseas affiliate and sent to the head office so that a consolidated world-wide exposure can be produced. For example, if one unit is over-sold Swiss francs against the US dollar and another unit is over-bought Swiss francs against Deutschmarks, then the whole bank's exposure is, if the amounts are equal, an over-bought US dollar position and an over-sold Deutschmark position. Depending upon the bank's policy, this may be the bank's total foreign exchange position or just the dealer position; if the latter, then to obtain the bank's complete foreign exchange position in a particular currency, such items as capital or tax exposures (if in a foreign currency either unhedged or not funded locally) must be added to the dealer position.

Because monies are flowing in and out in so many currencies on different days, some form of cash flow or liquidity report is required in order to monitor the action required in the future. The degree of detail depends upon whether the report is for dealer use, local management or head office management consolidation. Such a report comprises three parts:

(a) The net cash in or out for a particular period resulting from deposit activities.
(b) The net cash in or out for a particular period resulting from interest arbitrage activities (deposit, loan and foreign exchange combined).
(c) The net cash in or out for a particular period resulting from forward foreign exchange activities.

The report might appear as per Figure 7.2—the columns have been labelled A–J for reference. It is usual for the net movement of money to be preceded by a plus sign if funds are to be received and by a minus sign if funds are to be paid away.

The total amount of deposits placed or lent would be entered under their maturity date in columns A and B. If the start date was after the date of the report then it would need to be included twice—once under its commencement date and once under its maturity date. Also to be included in column B would be commercial loans entered either by their maturity date if a fixed rate commitment, or under their roll-over date if a floating rate loan. Column C would then be used in one of two ways—either to show the net cash in or cash out for a particular period or the cumulative effect of all such inflows or outflows. This method of reviewing the interest rate risk for roll-over loans is only satisfactory for assessing the exposure from a change in rates. A second liquidity report should also be regularly produced showing the loans under their final maturity and not under their roll-over date, in order to show the possible funding risk. In order to be conservative, negotiable assets should not be shown as a liquid asset but should be entered under their maturity date. Capital is regarded as the most stable money and the least likely to be withdrawn. Conversely, demand accounts (current accounts or due-to accounts) are shown as the most unstable at the top of the report with funds due today for repayment. This is the most conservative method of recording the rate exposure.

Columns D and E are shown for purposes of explanation. Often such columns are combined with A and B since column E can distort the true position. For example, if all deposits have been taken in one currency and then sold and lent in another on a fully hedged basis, column E would show large maturities of deposits taken and no source of money to enable repayment to occur. Therefore, in this example, the deposit taken would

Cash flow/liquidity report as at . . . for [currency]

Period	Deposits taken A	Deposits placed B	Net position C	Foreign exchange sold against deposits taken D	Foreign exchange bought against deposits placed E	Net deposit position F	Foreign exchange sold G	Foreign exchange purchased H	Net Foreign exchange position I	Net Foreign exchange and deposit J
Today										
Tomorrow										
Next day										
Day after										
Next 15 days to										
– „ –										
– „ –										
Next 3 months to										
– „ –										
– „ –										
Next 6 months to										
– „ –										
– „ –										
19. .										
19. .										
Capital										

Fig. 7.2 Sample cash flow liquidity report

appear in column A and the foreign exchange forward contract in column E. Thus, column E is the net deposit position on either a cash flow basis for a particular period or a cumulative over-lent or over-borrowed position when all periods are added together. In the example just cited, there is no foreign exchange position or cash imbalance.

Foreign exchange in and foreign exchange out are shown in columns G and H. The report in Figure 7.2 is for one currency: therefore, exchange purchased will show in column H on one report and column G on another currency report. The foreign exchange forward positions can be seen on a cash flow or cumulative basis in column I.

As has previously been explained, it is possible for all foreign exchange positions, provided there is no special exchange control restriction, to be covered either in the foreign exchange market or in the deposit market. Therefore, the bank's overall net dealing exposure is column J, which is columns F and I combined on either a cash flow or cumulative basis. Whilst dealers and local management are interested in the total report, it is column J which is the most important.

From individual currency reports a total exposure report can be produced as in Figure 7.3

Money market report as at . . .

Period	Currency A	Currency B	Currency C	Total*
Today				
Tomorrow				
Next day				
Day after				
Next 15 days to				

*Usually expressed in either dollars or local currency

FIG. 7.3 Sample money market report

The report shown in Figure 7.3 can be produced on a cash flow or cumulative liquidity basis.

If at all possible, and this usually means the use of a computer system, rates should be attached to the gaps or cash imbalances. These rates should reflect the rates or prices of the gaps or mismatches. It is then necessary to compare the prices with the current market and hence an indication will be obtained of potential or imputed profit or loss. These imputed rates can only be read as a guide or indication because of the many different ways in which a position can be covered.

In the previous chapter mention was made of the credit risk and the transfer risk. To monitor such risks, reports must be produced regularly to show the amount of money placed with either a particular counterparty or in a particular country and to show the amount of foreign exchange outstanding with one particular counterparty or country. Such reports should compare the actual figures outstanding with the previously established limits. During the day, control must be maintained so that new deals will not, when combined with the outstanding deals, exceed the previously established limits after allowing for maturities. Normally, dealing departments are not allowed to exceed limits without reference to management to see if any excess will be permitted.

A daily projection should be produced to show the net cash in or out for each correspondent bank account. This will enable appropriate action to be taken to ensure that no idle balances are left uninvested and that no correspondent bank account will be overdrawn or its balance so reduced that the amount remaining will not be enough to compensate the correspondent for the servicing costs of the account.

ESTABLISHMENT OF LIMITS

The amounts involved in any limit will, of course, vary from bank to bank depending upon the size, level of expertise and market activity of the bank concerned. Limits should be written guidelines approved by senior management after consultation with the dealing department and auditors. Such a written set of limits should include the following:

1. *Uncovered or Open Foreign Exchange Limit* The dealing department should be restricted as to how much it can in total be over-bought or over-sold in any one currency at the end of a trading day. It is also not uncommon for there to be an aggregate limit for all positions when added together, regardless of the sign. During the day such limits may be exceeded as banks execute or accept customers' orders. Because markets are volatile and losses

can just as easily occur during a day as overnight, a daylight limit is sometimes imposed. This is the maximum trading position which can be held at any time during the day.

2. *Gap Limits* These limits should restrict the amounts which can be over-lent, over-borrowed, over-sold or over-bought by currency in any one particular period or on a cumulative basis. Since it is often felt that the longer the period of exposure the greater the risk, such limits may vary with time, e.g. $50 million for up to one month, $30 million for up to three months, $20 million for up to six months and $10 million thereafter. They may also vary by currency as in some currencies with a limited market there is a greater risk than in currencies which enjoy large and active trading.

3. *Maximum Maturities* It is usual to find that individual counterparty credit limits for deposit placements or foreign exchange may only be used for periods of up to three months, six months, one year or such other period as may be decided upon. This is prudent, given that during the lifetime of a placement or foreign exchange contract the credit-worthiness of the counterparty may deteriorate. Money market activities are generally short-term to reflect the sources of deposit and the purpose, which is to help liquidity. If no time constraint applies, the bank could soon become very illiquid.

4. *Settlement Limits* These limits are easy to establish but can prove burdensome to monitor without a good computer system. They are none the less essential. As previously mentioned, on the day of settlement the risk in a foreign exchange deal is 100 per cent and of course the risk on the repayment of a deposit is 100 per cent. To limit this exposure, it is not uncommon for a settlement limit to be expressed as between 10 per cent and 25 per cent of the limit or as an absolute amount. This not only gives protection in the event of a bankruptcy but also, in the event of an operational error, it limits the potential overdraft charges to both the bank and the correspondent.

Daylight limits are sometimes imposed by correspondent banks or dealing departments. They are another type of settlement limit. Often a bank will ask for a large single payment or a large number of payments to be made on a particular day. Such payments are made by the correspondent, secure in the knowledge that, because of the stature of the counterparty, before the end of the day cover will have been provided. However, as was shown on 26 June 1974 with the Herstatt case, this is not always so and a risk can arise. A multiple of five times the settlement limit may be appropriate for a daylight limit.

5. *Parking Limits* In certain countries, it is not permitted to hold a position against a local currency in excess of a certain figure. Alternatively, some banks only permit foreign branches to keep nominal positions. In both these cases, positions, particularly foreign exchange over-bought and over-sold, are parked or placed with another unit. Where this practice is followed, it should only be done with head office as the unit to which the position is transferred and head office should have the right to close the position if it so wishes. It is a practice which, if not against the law in certain countries, may be against the spirit and, therefore, care should be exercised when considering any form of parking.

6. *Over-trading Limit* A bank is considered to be over-trading if it does not have the controls and administrative support necessary to support its volume of trading, if it is borrowing an excessive amount in the money markets, or if it is transacting such a large number of foreign exchange deals that it has reached the point where all potential lenders or dealers are at their own internal limits for that counterparty. Dealers as individuals are sometimes guilty of over-trading because of a wish to enhance their reputation in the market. The possible consequences of over-trading are various: perhaps the administrative support is not available and increased processing errors will occur; expenses may increase at a faster rate than the earnings; the bank may only be one way in the market and will have to pay a premium to obtain funds. As a control, a limit is sometimes placed on the total value of all outstanding forward foreign exchange contracts. If this figure is reached, then management's attention is drawn to the size of the dealing operation and a conscious decision can then be taken if it is necessary or desirable to increase the limit. A less practicable solution is to limit the number of trades per day.

7. *Individual Limits*
  (a) Specific credit limits will have been determined for each counterparty and country.
  (b) To cover the unexpected, specific limits are given to individuals so that they may approve a particular transaction. Limits might be a placement limit, a foreign exchange limit or an override limit. The amount of such limits will vary depending upon the size of the bank or branch and the level of expertise of the individual.

8. *Other Limits* Other limits which are often used to control activities might include the following:

  (a) Trades may only be permitted in certain approved currencies.
  (b) Limits as to the amounts of funds which are to be left overnight in nostro accounts.
  (c) Limits as to what type of deal, and under what conditions, a deal may be transacted with a maturity in excess of one year.
  (d) A written policy as to how option contracts are to be handled and covered.

REVIEW OF LIMITS

It is essential that all limits, such as those above, be reviewed on a regular ongoing basis. A bank will grow; market conditions will vary; customers and types of business will change; a chief dealer may leave—any of these can affect the practicability of the limits. Consequently, it may be necessary to increase or decrease any limit. In addition, it is possible that a limit is not being monitored carefully and a change in procedures is necessary. Limits should not be regarded as static or not subject to change.

Limits are written to protect the bank, its shareholders and depositors, but they must be written in such a way that a dealing department can operate and achieve its objectives.

An independent or internal auditor can be particularly helpful in assisting with the review of the monitoring of limits as well as in assessing their practicability. An auditor should ensure that the system is not only producing accurate and reliable information but also that it provides sufficient checks and balances to act as a control on as many types of fraud or error as possible. Independent verification of balances and outstanding contracts must be undertaken as well as selected testing of individual procedures. Periods spent by the auditor in the dealing department itself can often prove useful to ensure that a second set of books is not being maintained, that no kick-backs are being paid to the dealers by any customer or broker and that policies are being adhered to. An auditor may also notice if a limit is impracticable during such a visit. Audits should be of two types—ongoing and, from time to time, of a surprise nature.

MANAGEMENT

No matter how well written are the limits, how good an accounting system is in place or how practical the absolute numbers, they will not of themselves ensure that a profit is always made on every transaction and that large losses will never occur.

Communication between management and dealing department is vital. Regular (maybe daily) meetings should be held so that each can give the other the benefit of their advice. Opinions from customers, other bankers (both commercial and central), economists and politicians, must be obtained in order that a dealing strategy may be determined in view of the then prevailing economic and political situation. It is essential that both management and dealers try to keep fully abreast of market trends and views.

Losses will still occur from time to time but fortunately the reverse is normally true and a profit will be made. A thorough understanding of the problems involved in money trading will assist any manager who takes responsibility for such activities.

8 Profitability

As with any business enterprise, it is essential that the activity of the money dealing department be measured to see if it is profitable and making a worthwhile contribution to the overall profits of the bank. To do this, certain techniques are used. However, the assurance that the resultant profit is exactly apportioned cannot be given since, because of the nature of the interaction between foreign exchange and money market, some leakage between the two is inevitable.

REVALUATION OF FOREIGN EXCHANGE

It is only the exchange position which needs to be considered since any other realised profits or losses will have already been transferred to the profit and loss accounts.

The exchange position which must first be considered is that arising from foreign exchange trading. The most common method used to account for foreign exchange profits or losses is the closing rate method. In essence it is, acting on the assumption that were the bank to stop trading today and then to close all its exchange positions at the foreign exchange rates which then prevailed, what would be its resultant profit or loss? In other words, if it were long in a currency, would a profit or loss be made on the sale, and vice versa? The exercise is undertaken daily by banks actively engaged in the market and monthly or quarterly by those less actively involved.

At the end of each day, the spot rate of exchange for each currency in which the bank has a position will be obtained, either through the dealing department or independently as a control. At the same time, forward rates of exchange will be obtained for the regular value dates. Here, some form of interpolation is necessary. From these rates, either foreign exchange rates for every date on which the bank has foreign exchange exposure will need to be calculated manually or through a computer programme, or the exchange positions will have to be grouped into, say, half-month periods for convenience. For example:

EXAMPLE 8.1 Revaluation of Deutschmark exposure position for a bank which reports its profit/loss account in US dollars (+ = long position; − = short position)

Period		DM	US$ Equiv-alent	Current Market Rate	Value at New Market Rate	Profit/ Loss
Nostro balance	(A)	+ 100,000	− 50,000	1.9900	+ 50,251	+ 251
month 3	(B)	− 1,000,000	+ 498,000	1.9800	− 505,050	− 7,050
month 5	(C)	+ 2,000,000	− 1,025,641	1.9650	+ 1,017,811	− 7,830
month 6	(D)	− 2,000,000	+ 1,028,277	1.9600	− 1,020,408	+ 7,869
Net Position		− DM900,000	+ $450,636		− $457,396	− $6,760

The US dollar equivalent represents either the equivalent at the time of the transaction or the value as at the last revaluation. In Example 8.1 a loss of $6760 has occurred. Whilst the spot or nostro balance (A) shows a small profit, the three-month outright (B) is the element most contributing to the loss since to cover or close this position would today cost $7050. Therefore, a decision must be taken as to whether this loss should be realised now or whether the position should be held open in the expectation of the Deutschmark depreciating below 2.008 before the maturity date of the contract and a profit being obtained. The swap position (C) and (D) shows that whilst the actual outright rates of exchange have changed since the last revaluation, the differential shows little change. Therefore, the loss on one revaluation is offset by a profit on the other. This is always true since, as explained in Chapter 2, it is the differential which is of importance, not the actual rates of exchange. A profit or loss on a swap position will only occur if the differential moves.

To complete the revaluation, a debit (the loss) will be made to an exchange loss or income account. The contra-entry will be to write down the US dollar equivalents by $6760. If a profit had arisen, the reverse entries would have been made. For the trader, it is now the revalued figure which is important since it is on this figure that the value of the position must be recalculated and all future decisions made.

INTEREST ARBITRAGE

As will be recalled, a pure interest arbitrage transaction will comprise four parts: a deposit taken; a deposit or loan placed; a spot foreign exchange contract and a forward foreign exchange contract. The transaction will also only be entered into to produce an interest profit, *not* an exchange profit, and does not, or should not, leave an exchange exposure.

The profit/loss should be handled in the following manner. The interest expense on the deposit taken should be accrued during the life of the deposit. The interest income on the deposit/loan placed should also be accrued during the life of the transaction. The exchange difference between the spot and forward foreign exchange transactions should be amortised over the life of the transaction and transferred to an interest income or expense account and not to the exchange profit/loss account. In this way, a distortion is avoided. If, for example, funds had been borrowed at 9 per cent p.a. for three months and swapped and lent in another currency for three months at 3 per cent, the deposit activity would show a loss of 6 per cent p.a. for the three months and the exchange profit or loss would fluctuate each time the forward side of the transaction was revalued. It is, therefore, necessary to identify and distinguish such swaps from normal foreign exchange trades. This is normally done by the dealer indicating on the dealing ticket at the time the trade is made that such a foreign exchange deal is part of an interest or deposit arbitrage and not a regular foreign exchange deal. If the foreign exchange deal is for an amount larger than the corresponding deposit/loan or is for a longer period, then it is not a pure interest swap and only part can be handled this way since the difference in amount, or gap, must be revalued.

At the time the transaction is commenced, interest expense will begin to accrue in one currency and interest income in another. This is an exchange position. A conscious decision must, therefore, always be made as to whether this position should be allowed to remain open or whether it should be closed by a forward contract to cover the interest exposure. It would be normal for the forward contract to be for the maturity date of the interest swap. Prudence should dictate that it is bank policy to cover such interest exposure, otherwise something similar to Example 8.2 could occur:

EXAMPLE 8.2

Deposit taken interest expense $360 over 3 months	= $120 per month
Deposit placed interest income SFcs 120 over 3 months	= SFcs 40 per month
Exchange difference profit $390 over 3 months	= $130 per month
Spot rate of exchange $/SFcs at commencement of deposit/loan swap $1	= SFcs 2

∴ Total envisaged profit at time deal was made

= Interest Income
− Interest Expense
+ Exchange Profit

$$= \left(\frac{120}{2}\right) - 360 + 390$$

= $90 or $30 per month

If at maturity of swap the rate of exchange $/SFcs is now $1 = SFcs 3, then:

$$\text{Actual Profit} = \left(\frac{120}{3}\right) - 360 + 390$$

$$= \$70 \text{ or } \$23.3 \text{ per month}$$

In Example 8.2 the translation of the actual Swiss francs received into dollars was at a worse rate of exchange than at the time the contract was consummated. Consequently, instead of making $90 or $30 per month which had been accrued in the accounts, only $70 was made. As a result, the last month's income would be for $10, being the difference between the $60 accrued (2 ×30) and the $70 received. In practice, such distortions occur daily or monthly and not just at the maturity date. Thus, income is always being affected unless a forward transaction has been consummated to provide a known rate of exchange for the interest payment/receipt. This is why the formula already discussed on p. 68 is so important, since it includes the effect of covering interest forward.

NEGOTIABLE INSTRUMENTS

Negotiable instruments can be handled in one of two ways depending upon the policy of the bank and the intent at the time of purchase. If at purchase it was intended to hold such negotiable instruments until maturity, then the income will usually be accrued over the life of the asset. If, on the other hand, the instrument is held with a view to trading prior to maturity, then it should be revalued and any resultant profit or loss taken into income. If the figure is a loss, the asset is written down to the revalued amount since this is the amount which would be realised on the sale of the asset.

ACCRUALS

To avoid distorting the profit and loss account and to match income with expense, it is normal practice to amortise interest paid and interest received over the life of the transaction. This will mean that, unless previously covered by a forward trade, such transfers of profit or loss for whichever currency in which they were made into the reporting currency will create a foreign exchange position. This position must be reported to the dealing department as it occurs and then be included in their foreign exchange position. As such, it will be revalued and a decision must be made as to whether or not to cover. If the position is solely an accrual and not representing the actual receipt or payment of cash, it would be normal to cover for a future date rather than a spot date. Interest income or expense is an important part of the total foreign exchange position and should be reported as such.

FASB 8

In discussions on measuring profitability, the Statement of Financial Accounting Standards No. 8 (FASB8) issued by the Financial Accounting Standards Board in the USA in October 1975 should be referred to since it imposes a specific set of rules on United States companies or on companies who are required to prepare accounts by United States authorities. In essence, FASB8 requires that all non-monetary balance-sheet items (inventories, carried-at-cost property, plant and equipment and intangible assets) which are used by a company's overseas subsidiary are to be translated into dollars at the historic rate of exchange which prevailed on the day the assets were acquired. All monetary items (cash on hand, accounts receivable, debts and accounts payable) must be translated at the current rate of exchange prevailing at the date of the report. This has currently led to much comment and criticism with the depreciation of the US dollar during 1977 and 1978. It has also led to increased foreign exchange hedging by corporations or borrowing in local currencies to match assets in the same currency.

EVALUATION OF PROFITS/LOSSES

This is perhaps one of the most difficult problems—how to evaluate the results of a dealing department. Some banks regard their dealing department as a service or cost centre, others regard it as a profit centre, and there are others who look to the dealing activity to generate a large proportion of the institution's total earnings.

Because the currency markets are so volatile, it is perhaps unwise to regard dealing departments as a steady and ever-increasing source of income. In some periods exceptional profits will be obtained but, equally, in others large losses will also undoubtedly occur. Sometimes the establishment of too aggressive a profit target can result not only in the taking of large positions and an unacceptable level of risk but also in large losses or swings in profits.

In evaluating the profits, reference should be made to the individual bank's reasons for having a dealing department. For example, if it is solely to satisfy customer orders and to cover its expenses, perhaps the dealing department will make no profit, whereas the bank will benefit from customers increasing the size of their deposits because they are pleased with the service they have received. Another bank may view it as part of its advertising budget since a dealing department may be expected to be active to cover its costs and overheads but make no positive contribution to profits. However, by being active and gaining the reputation as a market-maker, it may find it easier to obtain deposits, either interest-bearing or interest-free, or it may be the only way to commence business with a prospective customer, the hope being that once some business has been transacted other and more profitable business will follow.

The examples just quoted might be extreme but they do illustrate the problem of evaluation of foreign exchange dealing. Unfortunately, the evaluation of foreign exchange earnings is a very inexact science and whilst a few banks will disclose their earnings from foreign exchange, none will disclose the amount of profit in relation to turnover, amount of forward contracts outstanding or average size of position taken during the year. Similar dilemmas exist in evaluating the deposit taking and placing activity. If the sole purpose is to service the bank's liquidity, it could be argued that the function of the dealing department is, after covering overheads, to break even, since to a bank this is a cost of doing business and the profit should be obtained elsewhere.

Whatever the reason for its existence, a dealing department should cover its costs. Therefore, a detailed analysis of the cost of a transaction should be undertaken so that some yardstick can be obtained. This expense, multiplied by the number of transactions, should be deducted before any further consideration of profitability.

There is little agreement as to the value of forward contracts which a bank should have outstanding in relation to capital. In only a few countries (and this is really only since the Herstatt case) has any regulation been imposed by a central bank limiting the level of foreign exchange activity to capital. If the level of risk in a foreign exchange contract is 20 per cent of the nominal value, perhaps such a figure should not exceed five times capital. However, the risk of a default does not, in reality, extend to all contracts but only to a small percentage, so a very large multiple is possible. Twenty to one might be considered as a target maximum for the ratio of a bank's earning assets to capital. Of these earning assets, perhaps some 10 per cent to 15 per cent might be held in redeposits. If the return on capital pre-tax is expected to be at least 15 per cent to 16 per cent then perhaps a spread on redeposits of .35 per cent to .45 per cent might be appropriate. If the earning asset to capital ratio is higher than twenty to one then perhaps a return of .2 per cent p.a. is acceptable in order to give the same return on capital. Therefore, some level of target spread should be established for any particular dealing department.

Profit should, therefore, be commensurate with the risks involved, the overheads and the level of outstanding business. A comparison is often difficult because, in some centres only exotic or little-used currencies will be traded and margins tend to be wide, whereas in other centres high activity in currencies with little spread between bid and asked rates is needed to generate the same level of income.

Finally, perhaps the following numbers might be useful:

A 1/8 % p.a. change in the rate of interest means a change in income of $125,000 per $100 million of deposit exposure.

A 10 cent change in the value of the $/SFcs means approximately $500,000 per $10 million of exposure.

Therefore, perhaps a greater exposure in positions is justified in the money market activity compared with the foreign exchange activity since the risk of a loss is perhaps not so large.

9 The Dealer

What are the requirements for being a good foreign exchange or money market dealer? There is a saying that a dealer is born not made, and the motto of the Association of Foreign Exchange Dealers (Forex Club) is 'Once a Dealer always a Dealer'.

Anyone who wishes to become a dealer must be of the highest integrity since he will hold a position of trust and responsibility with the organisation. Once qualified, he is responsible for the buying, selling, lending and borrowing of large sums of money on behalf of the bank and its customers. At no time must there ever be the temptation to deal for himself. This has happened in certain organisations with disastrous results.

A person wishing to become a dealer should possess a lively and enquiring mind. Because of the speed of the movement of exchange and money market rates, the ability to think quickly and positively is important. A decision has to be made by the dealer himself or by one of his colleagues in the dealing department as to whether or not to undertake a particular trade. Indecision will cost money. Therefore, he must be capable of assuming responsibility for his actions.

A dealer could, and does, come from any background. An understanding of economics is helpful but not essential to commence training. Often even a senior dealer has little understanding of macro or microeconomics but trades against an immediate reaction to economic headlines and in practice this reaction is what initially moves markets. Once accepted as a trainee, he must try to learn as much of the theory as possible— why do exchange rates move; what is the interaction between deposit rates of interest and forward rates of exchange; what does central bank intervention mean; what will be the effect on the exchange rate if inflation, money supply and balance of payments deficits are increasing?—and so on.

Because of the involvement with figures, an aptitude for mathematics is looked for when hiring a dealer and, as mentioned, an enquiring mind. He is expected to make his own decisions and not be led, for example, by brokers. It is unacceptable for a dealer to have a wrong or loss-making money position and to offer as the excuse that somebody else told him it looked all right. If the dealer took a view on a currency, was wrong but can explain why that view was taken, then an analysis can be made of what went wrong and why, and a lesson learnt.

Case studies and simulated dealing teach-ins are a very helpful method of assisting a dealer's training. Such courses should also include reference to operations department paper flows, central bank requirements and revaluation techniques since a good dealer must possess awareness of what both the volume and type of transaction may mean to another area of the bank or its balance sheet. Many banks insist that all potential dealers work in an operations department for a period of time in order to gain this understanding.

If an individual shows that he possesses the makings of a good dealer then some form of cross-border exposure will be very useful. Such experience in another centre can certainly assist in developing a language ability which is of use to a money trader since not only can foreign-language newspapers and periodicals be read in order to gain an added insight into how and why a currency's rates may move, but this knowledge of a language can also help in marketing, developing new contacts and facilitating transactions which are themselves cross-border, thus lessening the risk of error. Experience in another country is also useful in that the dealer can obtain a specialised knowledge of a particular currency or market, which can then not only give the institution a competitive edge in the market but can also assist a particular customer. A worthwhile side-benefit to the individual dealer and to the institution of such a cross-country training is that contacts or friendships can be established which will stand all concerned in good stead in future years. For example, if a currency is moving erratically, it is always advantageous to be able to contact a friend for an unbiased opinion which, based on past experience, is known to be reliable.

Not only must the dealer be intelligent, dependable and competent, he must also be capable of working as a member of a team. Individuals who cannot accept this discipline will probably not make good dealers. Markets are related; one trader must work with another in informing the other as to what is happening and why so that each may be aware of what the effect will be on their own position, be it foreign exchange or money market. Rarely is one trader capable of doing everything and such input is therefore vital. The successful dealing manager is aware of this and should try to mould the traders into a team so that profit opportunities are recognised. The most successful dealing departments tend to be those where individuals work closely with each other.

Business is often based on some form of dealing, be it the shopkeeper who buys from a wholesaler at one price to on-sell to the customer at a different price, the customer who borrows from a bank at one rate of interest because he knows that the funds can be employed more profitably in his business, or the manufacturer who produces goods at one price and expects to sell at another which will produce a profit. This being so, many banks insist that all management trainees spend some time working in a dealing environment as part of their general training and so have a better understanding, not only of the foreign exchange and money markets, but also of business.

Dealers themselves often become specialists in either foreign exchange or liability management as their careers develop. As foreign exchange rates fluctuate, so an awareness of the impact on a bank's capital risk in a foreign country and currency is needed by management. With increasing pressure on lending margins and operating expenses in banking, successful liability management is often the key to increasing profits. Thus, with a good dealing department background, a very worthwhile career is possible.

Dealers must recognise that a very high standard is expected of them. Because of the nature of trust, a dealer must at all times stand by a commitment made to a customer or another banker no matter what the consequences to him personally. A dealer must maintain the confidentiality of his trades and should also recognise the responsibility owed to the bank. Therefore, not only must the policies, limits and procedures of the bank be adhered to but also all irregularities, either within the dealing department or market, must be reported to the bank's management.

The progress of a dealer is normally from a position as a trainee dealer to that of a dealer, then senior dealer and manager. In other words, it is similar to an apprenticeship with much of the training coming on the job supplemented by theoretical and formal training.

The Euro-market is comparatively young but the profession of dealing is old. Therefore, whilst the principles remain the same, the complexity of the market is increasing. As a consequence, it is conceivable that dealers in the future will have to have a higher level of formal academic training than has been the case in the past. An ability to communicate concisely and effectively with the customer and management is also going to become more and more important as the complexity of the markets increases.

10 Particular Customers

It is important for anyone involved with the foreign exchange and money markets to try to understand the influence of central banks on the market. A central bank has the following amongst its responsibilities:

1. To act as banker to the government.
2. To act as lender of last resort.
3. To assist in executing the government's economic policy by influencing the total supply of credit and the level of short and long-term interest rates and by maintaining the value of the currency at an agreed level.

Because of the above, central banks can constitute a very large proportion of the total turnover in the market. A dealing department can view a central bank as either a potential source of profit or a source of information about future trends, or both. Governments establish policies and preferences and a change in either can alter the value of an exchange rate or the level of interest rates. For example, is it government policy to have stable exchange rates, improved balance of payments, lower interest rates, an increase in the standard of living, lower inflation, or full employment? If the priorities change, so too will the rates.

In one-way markets of all sellers or all buyers of a currency, the central banks are sometimes the only counterparty willing to trade the opposite way. As such, central banks and dealing departments often make their profits at different times. For example, the central bank may decide to hold a rate of exchange at a given level and will, therefore, buy unlimited amounts of local currency at this price in exchange for a foreign currency. A dealing department then has a support price and can buy unlimited amounts of local currency from its customers and on-sell to the central bank, secure in the knowledge that it will not make a loss should the exchange rate change during the transaction. One-way markets occurred in 1967 when the Bank of England bought unlimited amounts of sterling in exchange for foreign currency prior to the devaluation of the pound. Another example could be a country with a cyclical balance of trade in that during the first half of the year it imports more than it exports and during the second half the reverse occurs. Under these circumstances, a central bank will often support the rate of exchange to ensure that there will be a stable market throughout the year which will not be subject to special purchase or sell orders caused by the trade cycle.

Dealing departments need to try to estimate the extent of official intervention since this is often a guide to the level of pressure on a currency. The absence of pressure of official intervention can also be a clue to the aims of government policy or the likelihood of a change in official priorities.

Central banks regularly contact the dealing departments of commercial banks to obtain information as to whether there is a large pressure building up in a particular currency or whether there are large sell or buy orders at that moment. Central banks also like to trade from time to time in the foreign exchange markets, not because of a wish to intervene but because they wish to take a sample of whoever is the current market-maker and see if that particular bank or counterparty is fulfilling its obligations correctly—e.g. is its operations department in order; do confirmations arrive in time; are payments effected correctly? From such random sampling or questioning, central banks are able to detect if perhaps a bank is over-extended or over-trading, either of which could lead to a bank failure which could have further repercussions on the banking system.

Some central banks place deposits in the Euro-markets directly, some operate through the Bank for International Settlements in Basel (the Central Bankers' bank), some deal directly with another central bank and still others may do all three. Whichever option they take, central banks are an important source of large stable interest-bearing deposits for a commercial bank. Dealing departments should note, therefore, for what maturities such funds are being placed as sometimes this can indicate a possible movement in interest rates. By way of an example—if a particular central bank is placing deposits with a long maturity, it may indicate either that there is a wish to hold down the level of long-term interest rates, or that interest rates are about to fall. Conversely, a central bank can glean something about the bank's position or policy if it notes that the bank in question is bidding aggressively for funds in a particular period. This could indicate that the bank is either short of funds or is anticipating an increase in interest rates.

Traders should try to understand the possible effects of central bank intervention in the markets. If there is pressure for an appreciation in a currency then dealers will be buying the currency which it is thought might revalue and selling that which will devalue. As funds are bought, and if the final seller is the central bank, the money supply might increase. Additionally, the funds purchased need to be deposited and so interest rates may fall. This may not suit government policy and, therefore, it may be necessary to ban any further deposits of local currency by non-residents in the country.

The central bank which is supplying the currency in demand is receiving another currency in exchange. A dealer should try to see what is happening to this money—for example, whether it is being used to purchase foreign government treasury bills. If this is the case then this action might well reduce that government's need to fund its budget deficit in the private market and so help keep down interest rates in that country, notwithstanding that its currency is weakening.

Central banks work closely together and as a result it is very rare indeed to arbitrage one against another in the same currency.

Apart from supporting the spot rate of exchange at an acceptable level, or supporting an agreement such as the EEC snake, the central banks use the forward markets. By supporting a forward outright rate of exchange, a central bank can preserve the spot level since the difference between the two should equal the interest differential. The purchase of the forward local currency under pressure means that the central bank does not immediately have to part with its foreign exchange reserves. Consequently, it can hope that by the time it has to settle the forward contract, it will have sufficient funds. If it does not have the funds then it will have to borrow from the International Monetary Fund, from other central banks or the Bank for International Settlements, arrange a reciprocal swap facility with another foreign central bank, increase interest rates and hope to attract private funds, or borrow abroad itself or through the encouragement of private long-term borrowing. A dealing department should watch to see which method is used since it could influence interest rates or exchange rates and thereby produce a profit or loss to the bank and its customers.

Recently, forward foreign exchange intervention has been very widely used by central banks to support their currencies. This has been either on an outright or swap basis. The aim is to try to move the forward swap differential or outright price in such a way that a covered interest arbitrage will result in a profit to the arbitrageur. For example, if the Swiss franc is under pressure to revalue, the central bank can reduce the cost of the swap (the percentage per annum cost of the forward differential) such that an arbitrageur can, by borrowing Swiss francs, selling them spot for US dollars, investing the US dollars and selling them forward for Swiss francs, produce a profit. In this way the inward flow of funds for an appreciation will be offset by an outflow of funds in the arbitrage. Thus the danger of revaluation is reduced. Conversely, if the central bank wished to either force interest rates up or support a currency, it would increase the forward differential and thereby the swap costs.

Central banks are in a unique position—they have advance knowledge of government policies and statistics; they have large resources and can intervene at will. In theory then, the advantage always lies with the central bank, not with the dealer at the commercial bank. However, as history has shown with the pound, the yen, the dollar, the French franc and the Spanish peseta etc., a central bank can only slow down the inevitable result of market pressure or stabilise a market. If the underlying economic situation of a country is weak, a depreciation in value will sooner or later be necessary. Similarly, if the economy is strong with a healthy balance of payments and low inflation, an appreciation is inevitable. Because of the outflow of reserves, it is normally easier to predict and force a depreciation than an appreciation.

THE LARGE MULTINATIONAL

Another major customer of a bank's dealing department is the large multinational company. Such a company is transacting business in a great number of different countries, dealing with a variety of currencies from the major to the exotic and manufacturing and/or selling a diverse range of products. As a consequence, it is not possible to generalise on their common approach to the problems of protecting their foreign exchange position.

Since the breakdown of the Bretton Woods system of fixed parities, such companies have become more and more exposed to the potential losses and/or profits which can occur through the movement of a foreign exchange rate. Traditionally, the US dollar, the Deutschmark and the Swiss franc were strong, the Brazilian cruzeiro, the Argentine peso and the pound sterling were weak. Therefore, all company treasurers operated in a similar manner, i.e. they invoiced only in a strong currency, they limited capital exposure in these countries and they moved retained earnings out of a weak currency into a strong currency as quickly as possible.

With exchange rates now floating and with the impact of FASB8, more and more international and multinational companies have had to consider the effects of rate movements on their balance sheets and their profit and loss figures.

Exceptional items in the company's income statement resulting from exchange rate movements tend to be a combination of two types of profit or loss. The first is an actual or realised profit or loss. Such a profit or loss might occur if a company invoiced a buyer in a foreign currency and upon receipt and conversion into the local currency made either an actual foreign exchange profit or loss compared with the estimated amount to be received at the time of sale. The nature of this exposure varies from company to company. For example, a trader may only have to worry about a period of 90 days compared with a company involved in the construction of capital projects which may have such an exposure for a five-year period.

The second type of exceptional profit or loss may result from a revaluation which may have been performed by the company either in accordance with local practice or with FASB8 rules. The resultant figure of a profit or loss will, at this stage, be an unrealised or theoretical number. Such a profit or loss will only occur if the exposure is realised by the sale or purchase of actual currency to cover the revaluation figure. A large part of a company's foreign exchange exposure is in fixed assets and inventory. If on one quarterly reporting date the value of the inventory has declined due to a fall in the value of the currency, the company treasurer is faced with the decision whether to cover this depreciation by actually selling the currency forward to protect the exposure, or to do nothing in the belief that the depreciation in the value of the currency is only temporary and by the next quarter date the currency will have appreciated.

Most company policies are such that they aim to derive their profit from the sale of their product, not from exchange rate movements. As such, multinational companies try to minimise the effect of foreign exchange movements on their balance sheets and income statements. Since the advent of FASB8 has heightened the awareness of the investor in currency fluctuations, there has been a noticeable increase by US corporations in foreign exchange transactions at the approach of a quarterly reporting date. Also, many companies, not just those in the United States, have increased their borrowing in the weak currencies and prepaid their borrowing in the stronger currencies. Such awareness has led to increased communication between the dealing departments of banks and the treasury departments of corporations. Companies seek advice from their bankers as to the likely trend of a currency. They also seek opinions and guidance as to the best method of protecting their exposure. The banker must try to understand each particular customer's needs since each will vary.

A company which has in place a good foreign exchange exposure reporting system is obviously better placed to discuss this exposure with the bank than one without. Consequently, banks sometimes offer as a service a programme to produce such a report in order to be better placed to advise the corporation. Once the level and amount of exposure has been determined, the next question is—for when shall cover be effected? A multinational company is an ongoing business so such a question must be continually asked. Also, because forecasting exchange rates is not an exact science where predictions can be made as to rate movements which vary hourly, daily, or monthly depending upon whose advice has been sought, there is always an element of risk in effecting such cover as exchange rates do not always move as predicted.

Corporations have a variety of methods which they can adopt to protect their foreign exchange exposure. If local assets are matched exactly with local liabilities in the local currency or if all sales and invoices are made in the local currency, there is no risk of any profit or loss resulting from foreign exchange rate movements. Unfortunately, this is not always practicable and besides it would be naive to suppose, if there were a way of taking either a currency exposure or of covering to produce a profit, that it would not be done. Specifically, the corporation could undertake a forward transaction with the bank, lead or lag on payments, increase or decrease local currency borrowing, change the investments of a company from one currency to another as well as vary the type of asset, and increase or decrease the parent company's capital exposure by reducing net worth, or requesting increased dividends, royalties, management fees etc.

The following technique is sometimes used by companies when selling in a convertible currency with an active forward market to either increase their profit margin or reduce the price of their product so that it becomes more competitive:

EXAMPLE 10.1

A UK company is trying to sell 100 widgets at $10 each.
Terms of trade: 180 days settlement.
At time of sale, spot $/Stg: $2 = £1.
5 months forward outright $/Stg: $1.75 = £1.

(a) If sale is successful at $10 per widget then in six months time $1000 will be received. If $10 gave the company a profit at the spot rate of $2 = £1, then the profit will be increased by selling $1000 forward to the bank since $1000 at 1.75 = £571 compared with £500 at the spot rate. The company has, therefore, made an additional £71 profit or 28 per cent.

(b) If there is resistance from the buyer at $10 per widget and if the UK company wants to receive £500 for the 100 widgets in six months' time, then the price can be reduced if forward cover is again undertaken, since:

$$\text{UK Price in } £ = \frac{\text{US price in } £}{\text{Forward Rate of Exchange}}$$

$$\therefore £500 \times 1.75 = \text{new US price for 100 widgets}$$
$$= \$875$$

∴ Each widget could be reduced in price to $8.75 and still leave the UK exporter with his original profit margin.

Whilst multinational companies undertake covered interest arbitrage transactions, they are sometimes, either by choice or because there is no viable alternative, left with an uncovered interest arbitrage transaction. In this case it is important that the break-even rate of exchange is calculated at the outset of the transaction and a decision made as to the likelihood of such a rate arising. It is often tempting to borrow in the cheapest currency, i.e. the one with the lowest rate of interest, and to invest in the dearest, i.e. the one with the highest rate of interest. Such policies can have disastrous effects on the balance sheet if not matched with a corresponding asset or liability, or income or expenditure in the currency chosen. None the less, such transactions can be profitable and attractive if used carefully. For example:

EXAMPLE 10.2

A company can borrow (a) the equivalent of $1 million in Swiss francs for one year at 3 % p.a.
or (b) $1 million for one year at 10 % p.a.
Current spot rate of exchange: $1 = SFcs 2

∴ Interest on SFcs 2 million at 3 % p.a. for one year = SFcs 60,000 = $30,000

∴ Interest on $1 million at 10 % p.a. for one year = $100,000

∴ If the company can borrow Swiss francs for one year at 3 % p.a., sell them spot and buy dollars, and at maturity of the loan can sell US dollars to purchase Swiss francs to repay the loan, and if the exchange rate has not changed from $1–SFcs 2, then a saving of $70,000 in interest costs has been achieved. However, the exchange rate could have moved to 1.8454 before the transaction became unprofitable for, as long as the Swiss franc principal plus the Swiss franc interest divided by the break-even exchange rate is less than the dollar principal plus the dollar interest, a saving will occur.

∴ $$\frac{2,000,000 + 30,000}{\text{Break-even exchange rate}} = 1,000,000 + 100,000$$

∴ Break-even exchange rate $= \dfrac{2,030,000}{1,100,000}$

$$= 1.8454$$

The corporation must now decide on the likely appreciation of the Swiss franc and whether or not this is a risk worth taking.

Examples 10.1 and 10.2 have illustrated methods by which a multinational company could use the foreign exchange markets and money markets. In all probability the counterparty for the company would be a bank's dealing department and, therefore, a bank would have to decide how best to cover its own position. None the less, the multinational would have provided the bank with the opportunity to make a dealing profit and the bank would have noted the details of the transaction. If a large enough sum is dealt for or if a large number of customers operate in a similar manner, the rates of exchange and interest will change. Therefore, the bank with the order will be the first to note the probability of the change and can cover its positions first.

The multinational company will often use the covered interest arbitrage techniques to provide capital for a subsidiary or to move temporary surplus funds from one subsidiary to another which is in deficit. To do either, the company, like a bank, must have a complete monetary and accounting system to record the nature of the transaction and its profitability.

On occasions, a company will not use a bank for forward cover since there may be a government scheme for covering the exchange risk. Alternatively, companies can net their foreign exchange exposures in inter-company dealings to eliminate the risk and reduce the cost, since the bank as an intermediary is eliminated. It should also be realised that because of tax, legal, exchange control or other similar considerations, it may not always be possible for the company to cover its exchange exposure as it might wish. Therefore, consultation with the bank's dealing department is useful to determine if there is a viable alternative.

11 Characteristics of Various Money Markets

Preceding chapters have dealt with the history of the markets and the theory and practice of foreign exchange and money markets. Whilst the same principles apply all over the world, every individual foreign exchange or money market has certain peculiarities either because of its location, the currencies handled, local exchange control, reserve requirements or market practice. As a consequence, dealing departments vary around the world with regard to the types and volume of transaction. The dealer, the money manager and the corporate treasurer, therefore, all need to have some knowledge of such peculiarities to see if one market is better suited than another to a particular transaction since that which can be undertaken in one centre may not be possible in another. Major centres include New York, London, Frankfurt, Zurich, Paris, Milan, Toronto, Bahrain, Singapore, Tokyo, Hong Kong, Amsterdam and Brussels.

THE FAR EAST MARKETS

The principal markets of the Far East comprise Singapore, Hong Kong and Tokyo. Markets in Australia and New Zealand exist but because of their restrictions on the opening of foreign banks' branches, relative geographic isolation, tight exchange control and limited use of their local currencies in international trade, they are not major centres.

Because of the importance of the value of the yen in international trade, Tokyo is potentially the most important of all the Far Eastern markets. Its growth as a major money centre in its own right has been hindered by the very tight exchange control regulations on the movement of yen into and out of the country, combined with a restrictive policy towards foreign banks' activities in the country. Recently the yen has become one of the five most actively traded currencies. The money market is dominated by the city banks and local brokers. Because of the time difference between Japan and the rest of the world, direct trading is possible only by the placing of best orders with branches or by banks in another centre working outside normal working hours. Development of the market as an international centre has been hampered by the tight exchange control conditions imposed by the Bank of Japan and by the imposition of withholding tax on deposits placed in yen in Japan. Interest on Eurocurrency deposits is usually paid gross or free of any tax deduction.

In the early 1970s, the Government of Singapore recognised that there was a need for an offshore currency market to develop in the region and accordingly it encouraged the development of the Asian dollar market. Foreign banks were solicited to open in Singapore to deal only in foreign currencies. Their activities in local Singapore currency were restricted and accordingly they received offshore banking licences. As an important trade entrepôt, Singapore had a need for the development of the money and foreign exchange markets. It was ideally situated as 'the crossroads of the East'. Whilst its deposit activity has grown rapidly, its foreign exchange growth has been somewhat slower. This is a result of the relative thinness of the market, as it has still only a limited number of active participants, and because of the isolation caused by the time difference between itself, Europe and the United States. None the less, as a deposit market for Eurocurrencies, it is probably the most important in the area. The market was fashioned upon European ideas as to practice, ethics and types of business which can be transacted.

Hong Kong is probably a more important foreign exchange centre than Singapore, but because of tax restrictions and the limited growth of foreign branches of banks its growth as a money market centre has been slower than Singapore. Nevertheless, as an important centre for commerce, it has a good base for future development. Like Singapore, it too is very much modelled along the lines of the London market.

Taken as a group, the three centres are important as sources of funds, users of funds and traders in foreign exchange. Their problem is the thinness of the market resulting from their relative size and newness. Consequently, a trend in a currency can become exaggerated and is often reversed when the much larger and older European market commences work which, due to the time difference, is towards the end of the working day in the Far East.

THE MIDDLE EAST MARKETS

Since the recent escalation in oil prices and the increase in wealth of the OPEC states, the Middle East has increased in importance as a source of Eurocurrency deposits. Traditionally, the deposits have been held in Eurocurrencies such as dollars, Deutschmarks, Swiss francs, pounds and yen. This has meant that the owners of the deposits have had a foreign exchange position against their own local strong currencies. Recently, loans have been arranged in local currencies for borrowers who are either willing to take an uncovered exchange risk or who will be receiving income in the local currency for goods sold or services rendered. As a consequence, the market in Saudi rials is expanding but it is still at an early stage of development.

Beirut used to be the financial centre for the Middle East but after the Intra Bank affair, and as a result of the civil war, its importance has declined and the newly emerging centre is Bahrain, where in 1977 deposits of offshore banks rose by 150 per cent from the 1976 figure to $15.7 billion.

Bahrain is conveniently situated between Europe and the Far East both geographically and in terms of time-zone. It is, therefore, a useful link in the twenty-four-hour money markets of the world. Expertise is at present largely imported and the market is still developing. Much of the deposits of the Middle East are not handled through Bahrain but are placed directly in London, Zurich, Amsterdam, Frankfurt, Paris, New York or Toronto.

The notable feature of the Middle East money market is that it is probably responsible for slightly in excess of 50 per cent of all new Euro-deposits with an original maturity in excess of one year. Consequently, the market is important for bond issues and private placements where long or medium-term funds are required at fixed interest rates.

EUROPEAN MARKETS

London is still perhaps the largest international financial centre in the world. It is also an anomaly in that today it is largely an offshore banking centre in a highly taxed area. The market share of London banks in the Euro-markets (now estimated to be about 27 per cent) has declined since the 1960s, partly as a result of the growth of other centres, partly as a result of London affiliates and branches of US banks transferring more and more assets to their Caribbean branches, and partly because of recent currency fluctuations which have led the Japanese branches to decrease the activities of their London branches.

None the less, London still probably accounts for a greater proportion of Euro-business than any other centre. For several hundred years the City of London has developed as a financial centre and today it has a depth and range of markets which is perhaps unparalleled. As a consequence, it has a high degree of flexibility and expertise.

With the exception of the London discount market, the London foreign exchange and money market is a telephone and telex market since most transactions are handled through these media rather than as a result of direct contact. At the centre of the London market is the Bank of England and around it are the several hundred active dealing banks, money brokers, multinational companies and foreign counterparties. For bank-to-bank transactions in foreign exchange and deposits between authorised (approved by the Bank of England) banks in London, such trades are handled exclusively by authorised money brokers. In exchange for providing the rate service to banks and providing the counterparty, they are paid a fee (brokerage) by the bank. They do not maintain positions in a currency themselves.

The London money and foreign exchange markets all interrelate, be they the traditional discount market, the forward foreign exchange market, the inter-bank deposit market, the Certificate of Deposit market, the government securities market or the local authority bond market, such that the ability of the market to cope with new flows of funds is perhaps unrivalled except by New York.

Within the London foreign exchange market it is possible to deal for forward contracts up to five years, which is an unusual feature since many markets are limited in dealings to up to six months or one year.

After the US dollar, perhaps the second most actively traded currency is the Deutschmark. As a consequence, Germany is an important counterparty, but unlike the UK with just one centre,

London, Germany has several—Frankfurt, Dusseldorf, Munich, Hamburg, and Berlin. Whilst Germany has a broker system, it also has official fixings in each of these centres which take place at the local stock exchanges, the most important being Frankfurt, since this is the international financial centre of Germany. A 'fixing' is a physical meeting of bank traders and the Bundesbank (German central bank) at the stock exchange at a given time each business day. Buyers and sellers trade until such time as all orders are satisfied. At such time, a fix or official price is established for each of the major currencies relative to the Deutschmark. This price is used for official figures and historically by large and small corporations for transactions for that day. Nowdays, however, many large corporations choose not to deal at the fixing but to deal during the day. These fixings occur in other European centres such as Paris, Amsterdam and Brussels.

The largest market in Germany is the spot dollar/Deutschmark market but there is also an active forward market which trades for up to five-year maturities. Historically, much of this forward business was transacted in Dusseldorf because the local banks were in receipt of regular forward orders from the large German corporations located in the region. Nowadays, however, this is no longer the case because many of the banks have concentrated their foreign exchange dealing in Frankfurt. Because of tight regulations on the inflow of money to Germany and the limits imposed by the Bundesbank on mismatch deposit positions, the German market is essentially a foreign exchange market. Since 1974, after the Herstatt affair, such regulations have been increased in an attempt by the German authorities to limit foreign exchange speculation. The Euro-deposit activity of the German banks, and in particular the Euro-Deutschmark activity, is concentrated in Luxembourg where all the major German banks are established. As a result, Luxembourg is now the largest centre for Euro-Deutschmarks.

Luxembourg is also an important centre for the major Swiss banks. Switzerland has tried to limit the inflow of funds from non-residents by introducing a penalty rate of interest if balances owned by non-residents exceed certain agreed amounts which are varied from time to time. No such limit applies to deposits placed in Luxembourg which has banking secrecy laws and is, therefore, a useful vehicle for Swiss institutions.

Switzerland (in particular Zurich but to a lesser extent Basel,

Geneva and Lugano) is one of the financial capitals of the world with regular large inflows of deposits from residents of countries other than Switzerland. Unfortunately, it does not have a large money market and, as a result, the large Swiss banks are obliged to place most of their excess deposits outside Switzerland in addition to the surplus funds received from non-residents. Consequently, the banks are active placers of Eurocurrency deposits—at the end of 1977 they had some $139 billion placed— and are active dealers in the exchange swap markets. Swiss banks have to adhere to specific liquidity requirements in Swiss francs at the end of each month and quarter which are imposed by the National Bank. At such times this causes a tightness for Swiss francs in the deposit markets which is only alleviated by the action of the National Bank in supplying additional liquidity. Switzerland does not have a formal fixing but banks consult informally with each other by telephone each day to produce an official price common to all banks for small transactions with customers.

France, and in particular Paris, is a very active and important Euro-centre. The market is dominated by the large nationalised French banks. Each business day there is an official fixing at which the central bank is represented, but the importance and volume of business transacted at this fixing is declining as more and more banks' traders do most of their business from their offices. French exchange control is very onerous; in particular, it restricts the activities of domestic French banks in the lending of French francs to non-residents through the placing of deposits, the granting of loans or the swapping of foreign exchange. As a consequence, Paris is the centre for spot French franc business and Geneva is the centre for forward franc transactions with non-residents. The French market is similar to London in that much of the inter-bank activity is handled by brokers. Banks in France must regulate their Euro-loan roll-over activities as French liquidity requirements are quite severe.

NORTH AMERICAN MARKETS

The North American market is principally located in New York and Toronto, but centres such as Chicago, Boston, Detroit, Los Angeles, San Francisco, Dallas and Houston all have one or more active participant in foreign exchange and Eurocurrency deposits. The market is essentially one of telex and telephone—there is no official fixing. A large proportion of the business is handled by brokers, many of them with strong affiliation to European brokers. One of the noticeable characteristics of the North American market is that whilst the foreign exchange activity is handled and booked by the head offices of the commercial banks, the deposit activity is handled by the head office but booked in a Caribbean branch which is normally located in Nassau or Grand Cayman. The reason for this is that the US banks are able to lend and borrow Eurodollars which are not subject to US regulatory requirements. With the removal of lending restraints in January 1974, there has been a much closer relationship between domestic US dollar interest rates and Eurodollar interest rates as arbitrage is now easier to effect. As evidence, United States institutions are now probably the largest single buyers of Eurodollar Certificates of Deposit since the yield which is obtainable is often in excess of that which can be obtained from a domestic Certificate of Deposit with a similar maturity. The interest rate difference is also used in reverse by banks and corporations since, if they have access to domestic US dollars at a rate below the comparable Euro-rate, it will lessen their funding cost. European banks and treasurers will arrange domestic dollar credit lines, acceptance facilities, commercial paper facilities or tap the Federal Funds market in order to be able to arbitrage at the right time.

The New York foreign exchange market is extremely active when sharing a common time with Europe, and has become more so with New York brokers now being permitted to effect trades between banks in New York and overseas, but it is perhaps a little thin at other times of the day. Because of the close geographic proximity of the United States and Canada, and because of the sizeable trade between the two countries, the largest markets for US dollars against Canadian dollars will be found in New York, Toronto, Detroit and Chicago. Since Canadian banks have significant operations in New York, there is an active deposit interest rate arbitrage between the two countries. The New York market traditionally quotes locally in terms of so many cents of a US dollar equalling one unit of foreign currency, compared with European and Far Eastern centres which quote the number of units of the foreign currency equal to one US dollar.

With the development of sophisticated communications and

the increased overseas branching of foreign banks, the foreign exchange and Euro-markets are becoming twenty-four-hour markets. As a consequence, the West Coast of the United States is increasing in importance as the link in the time-zone between East and West, and its share of the market is increasing.

12 Conclusion and Outlook

The importance of the money-dealing function increased during the 1960s and 1970s and by June 1978 the Euro-market had grown to an estimated size in excess of $700 billion. Of this figure, about 78 per cent of all business is estimated to be transacted in US dollars. Consequently, one of the continuing problems for banks and institutions operating in the market is how to ensure a smooth and efficient transfer of funds in New York, which is where much of the final settlement occurs. Problems have arisen in the past caused by the high volume of payments and it is conceivable that much greater use will be made in the future of local US dollar clearings and direct computer dialogue to help solve the problem.

Along with the growth of the market, the average size of transaction has increased, as a result of which, should an error, fraud or failure occur, the potential size of the loss is that much larger. Therefore, banks and institutions engaged in money dealing must continually review their systems to ensure that they are, and will be, adequate to control the flow and size of business, otherwise the well-publicised losses of Herstatt, Lloyds Lugano, Crédit Suisse, Banque de Bruxelles and Franklin will not be the last.

As the deal size increases, so too does the risk that individual depositors may become too large for a particular bank since they represent a disproportionate percentage of a bank's total deposits. The risk is that if the deposits are withdrawn, the bank concerned may have difficulty in replacing such an amount and hence will fail. A sound caveat of banking is to continue to grow and at the same time diversify the deposit base. Consequently, banks in the future may well impose limits on the total amount of deposits which they will accept from a single source.

Communications have improved such that today there is really only one market for foreign exchange and Eurocurrency deposits throughout the world. At the same time, the number of participants has grown, with the result that the increased competitiveness has led to a reduction in profit margins from regular trading. Bank managements should not look upon foreign exchange as a tap which can be turned on at will to generate unlimited profits. The case of Franklin National Bank, New York, will bear witness to this statement. Therefore, growth should be steady, based on sound practices, handled so that related costs are kept under strict control, and monitored to see if a satisfactory return is being achieved.

Now that markets are truly world-wide and leading banks are trading somewhere in the world every minute of the day, it is vital that proper limits and controls are enforced since such operations become increasingly difficult to manage. Central banks have also shown their concern such that they now work much more closely together in exchanging information about banks located in their countries. If a bank, branch or affiliate fails in a foreign country, whose responsibility is it? The practice has been to look to the central bank of the country of the location of the head office but a difficulty occurs with banks with multinational shareholders.

Corporate customers are becoming increasingly sophisticated in their use of the foreign exchange and currency deposit markets and are demanding ever more of their bankers, particularly in the area of rate forecasts. It is doubtful if any forecast will ever be 100 per cent accurate, whereas it is sometimes possible to predict the correct trend. For a multinational client, determination of this trend is vital so that he can then implement a foreign exchange policy which will meet his particular requirements.

For as long as there is no single world currency and for as long as exchange rates float, there will be a need for dealing departments in banks and companies in order that they may profit from foreign exchange and interest rate movements and protect their exposure.

Bibliography

Charles A. Coombs, *The Arena of International Finance*

Bank for International Settlements, Annual Reports

British Bankers Association, *London as an International Banking Centre.*

Chase Manhattan Bank, *International Finance* (fortnightly)

Raymond G. F. Coninx, *Foreign Exchange Today* (Woodhead-Faulkner Ltd., 1978)

Andrew Crockett, *International Money—Issues and Analysis*, 1st ed. (Thomas Nelson & Sons Ltd., 1977)

The Economist, Financial Report

Paul Einzig, *A Textbook on Foreign Exchange*, 2nd ed. (Macmillan, 1969)

Paul Einzig, *Foreign Exchange Crises*, 2nd ed. (Macmillan, 1970)

Paul Einzig, *Parallel Money Markets*, (Macmillan, 1971)

H. E. Evitt, *A Manual of Foreign Exchange*, 7th ed. rev. R. F. Pither (Pitman, 1971)

Financial Accounting Standards Board, 'Accounting for the Translation of Foreign Currency Transactions and Foreign Currency Financial Statements' (October 1975)

A. T. K. Grant, *The Machinery of Finance and the Management of Sterling* (New York: St. Martins Press, 1967)

R. F. Harrod, *Reforming the World's Money* (1965)

International Currency Review, (London, bimonthly)

D. R. Mandich (ed.), *Foreign Exchange Trading Techniques and Controls* (American Bankers Association, 1976)

Morgan Guaranty Trust Company of New York – World Financial Markets (Periodical and Tables)

Heinz Riehl and Rita M. Rodriguez, *Foreign Exchange Markets*, 1st ed. (McGraw-Hill Inc., 1977)

J. Henry Schroder Bank and Trust Company, 'The Schroder Report'

Swiss Bank Corporation, 'Foreign Exchange and Money Market Operations'

Glossary

The following is intended as a guide to some of the vocabulary which has been used in the book. Many of the words will also be used in any discussion concerning money dealing.

Appreciation The increase in the value of a currency compared with another as a result of market pressures rather than as a result of official government action such as a revaluation.

Arbitrage The simultaneous buying and selling or lending and borrowing of the same currency in different centres at different prices or rates in order to obtain a profit.

Balloon repayment The repayment of all the principal of a loan together with interest due from the last interest period on a given date.

Bear A speculator who holds an over-sold exchange position or an over-lent deposit position in anticipation of either a currency depreciating or interest rates falling.

Bear squeeze Official intervention or market pressure to force a bear to cover the gap or reduce the exchange exposure at a loss.

Bid rate The price or rate at which the market-maker will either buy foreign exchange or accept deposits.

Broker An individual who works for a firm of brokers and whose role it is to act as an arranger or intermediary in concluding a foreign exchange or deposit transaction between two or more counterparties, usually banks. A broker does not normally maintain a position in exchange or deposits.

Broker's difference Fee paid by a broker to a bank which incurred a loss as a result of a misleading quotation by the broker or because a deal was not completed due to broker error.

Brokerage (broker's fee) The commission normally payable by both counterparties to the broker for arranging the transaction. The amount will vary by centre, currency and maturity.

Bull A speculator who holds an over-bought exchange position or an over-borrowed deposit position in anticipation of either a currency appreciating or interest rates rising.

Business day A day on which the transaction can be settled in the appropriate centre. If it is a deposit deal, only one centre is involved; if it is a foreign exchange deal, the two centres of the currencies dealt must be open.

Cable (1) The transmission of a message. (2) A US dollar/ sterling transaction in foreign exchange.

Call money Interest-bearing deposits repayable either on demand or after a period of notice, depending upon the terms of the contract.

Certificate of deposit (CD) A negotiable instrument issued by a bank payable to bearer. It will certify that the specified amount shown on the Certificate has been deposited with the issuer at a stated rate of interest. The Certificate will further state the date of repayment and how repayment will be arranged. If the maturity date exceeds one year (maximum allowed is five years), it will provide for interim payment of interest. CD's can, once issued, be split into small denominations by the issuing bank at the request of the owner.

Clearing house funds (1) US dollar cheques deposited with a regional clearing house in the United States. (2) Uncleared funds held in correspondent accounts by non-United States banks and customers.

Commercial paper Promissory notes, bearing only one signature, which are acceptable as money market instruments because of the quality of the issuer.

Confirmation The written contract sent to each other by the counterparties in a transaction in order to corroborate the deal.

Convertible currency A currency which can, without restrictions, be exchanged into another.

Correspondent bank A bank which either pays or receives money or performs some other service for another bank.

Counterparty The other party (individual or corporate) involved in any transaction.

Covered position with a maturity gap Where one convertible currency is purchased against the sale of the equivalent of another currency for either immediate or future delivery, and the former currency is simultaneously sold against the purchase of the equivalent of the latter currency for future delivery, but for a later value date.

Country limit (transfer risk limit) A limit established by a bank as to the maximum exposure by amount and/or maturity which it wishes to have in any one particular country for loans, bank placements, foreign exchange, etc.

Cross rate The rate of exchange between two currencies which are foreign to the local centre. Rates against United States dollars are not normally regarded as cross rates by dealers because all other rates are based on these quotations.

Credit limit Limit established by a bank as to the maximum amount of business which it wishes to have outstanding with any one particular counterparty.

Depreciation The decrease in value of a currency compared with another as a result of market pressures rather than as the result of official government action such as devaluation.

Discount (1) For foreign exchange: when the forward foreign currency is cheaper than a spot purchase of the same currency, the forward differential is said to be at a discount. (2) For loans: when the interest due is deducted from the principal amount at the beginning of the period and not charged at the end.

Discount rate The interest rate established to discount the loan.

Dollar/local currency [e.g. $/SFcs] Convention for expressing one dollar as being worth so many foreign currency units.

Eurocurrencies (Euro-deposits, external funds) Currencies which are owned and held on deposit by non-residents of the country of the currency concerned, e.g. Eurodollars, external pounds, Asian dollars, Euro-Deutschmarks etc.

Exchange control Regulations or restrictions imposed by a central bank on banks, regardless of country of ownership, which operate in the country of the central bank. Such limitations only restrict the bank's activities in the specific country of the central bank.

Exchange Position The net over-bought or over-sold exposure in a currency compared with the local currency or some other currency.

Exchange rate The price at which one foreign currency can be bought or sold and another purchased.

Federal funds [Fed. funds] Funds or money on deposit or held by the Federal Reserve Bank in the United States.

Fixed exchange rates Where currencies are given a fixed value in terms of another and only limited fluctuation is allowed.

Fixing Method of establishing an exchange rate for either official quotations and notices for that day or for certain customer orders. This only occurs in certain money centres.

Flat interest rate An interest rate expressed as a percentage with reference to time. This is often used in calculating fees payable.

Float Interest-free funds available between receipt and disbursement.

Floating exchange rate Where unlimited fluctuation (clean float) can occur in the rate of exchange of one currency compared with another. The market is subject only to demand and supply. If central bank intervention occurs to restrict movement then it is called a 'dirty float'.

Foreign exchange (1) The conversion of one currency into another. (2) The currency of any country but the local country.

Forward differential (forward margin) The amount by which the spot rate of exchange is adjusted to obtain the forward rate of exchange.

Forward exchange The dealing in foreign exchange for any date beyond the spot date. This can be a purchase or sale of the foreign currency.

Forward exchange rate The rate at which a forward contract is consummated.

Forward/forward (1) The purchase of one currency against another for a future date and the sale of the same currency against another for a further future date. (2) The commencement of a deposit or loan from a date after the normal spot date with a subsequent repayment date.

Future contract Same as Forward exchange

Gap The time which elapses before the elimination of either a swap foreign exchange position or a mismatch deposit position.

Hedge The protection of a foreign currency exposure either by a forward exchange contract or by borrowing in the local currency.

Inter-bank dealing (1) The buying and selling of foreign exchange. (2) The lending and taking of deposits between banks.

Interest arbitrage (1) Covered: The taking of a deposit in one currency, conversion into another, the making of a loan or deposit in this currency, and the simultaneous forward sale of the currency lent to obtain a higher return and have a fully hedged position. (2) Uncovered: The taking of a deposit in one currency, conversion into another, and the making of a loan or deposit in this currency. This results in a foreign exchange exposure.

Interest rate The payment as a percentage per annum for the use of the money.

N.B. Negative interest rates are possible (see Chapter 5).

Intervention When a central bank or other official institution enters the foreign exchange or deposit markets to influence or stabilise the price or supply of funds.

Leads and Lags The acceleration or deferment of the payment of a foreign currency debt.

Limit order An order placed by a customer with a bank, or by a bank with another bank, whereby in their absence the bank is instructed to execute a deposit or foreign exchange contract at either the 'best' price available or up to a certain rate. Such orders are normally only good for a specific amount and period.

Limits Rules and regulations imposed by a bank's management on its dealing room.

London interbank offered rate (LIBOR) The rate used in loan roll-overs and which is the rate of interest at which deposits were on offer or available in the London inter-bank market at a particular time for a particular period.

Long (1) To be over-bought in one currency against another. (2) To be over-borrowed in one currency.

Market-maker The counterparty who is requested for a foreign exchange or deposit price.

Maturity date (1) The settlement date for an exchange contract. (2) The date of repayment for a loan or deposit.

Mismatch Imbalance in cash flow either as a result of exchange or money market activity.

Money market [financial centre] A place where significant buying and selling of money occurs.

Nostro accounts (due-from accounts) Current accounts held by banks as working balances with their correspondent banks.

Odd dates Days which are not regular trading days in the money market and for which a quotation is requested in exchange or deposit.

Offer rate The price or rate at which the market-maker will either sell foreign exchange or place deposits.

Open position Gap or mismatch between value dates for either foreign exchange or deposits.

Options A forward foreign exchange contract for a precise amount of currency at a specific rate but with a variable settlement period instead of a fixed maturity date.

Outright   A forward purchase or sale of a currency.

Over-valuation   Currency is too expensive. The spot rate is over its purchasing power parity.

Parking   The placing of an exchange position with another unit of the same organisation.

Position   (1) The net over-bought or over-sold exchange position. (2) The mismatch position in forward exchange. (3) The mismatch position between deposits placed and taken.

Premium   When the forward foreign currency is more expensive than a spot purchase of the same currency, the forward differential is said to be at a premium.

Redeposits   The placement of interest-bearing, normally unsecured, deposits with other banks.

Reserve requirement   An obligation imposed on a commercial bank by a central bank to maintain a certain percentage of its deposits with the central bank.

Revaluation   (1) Similar to Appreciation. (2) Generally used when considering market value of outstanding forward contracts to determine profit or loss.

Revolving loan   When the loan is granted for a specific period but where it is subject to regular interest rate changes within this period.

Risk   The possibility of a loss, be it rate, credit or exchange.

Roll-over   (1) The date of changing the rate of interest on a revolving loan. (2) The extension or swapping of an existing forward contract.

Short   (1) To be over-sold in one currency against another. (2) To be over-lent in one currency.

Spot rate of exchange   Foreign exchange quotation for settlement two business days later.

Spot value   The date for settlement of a spot exchange deal. It is normally two business days from the date of contract.

Spread   (1) Difference between bid and offer rate in either exchange quotations or deposit quotations. (2) Margin obtained on redeposit trading.

Stand-in rate   Rate of interest or exchange which, whilst not the price of the transaction, reflects any accrued profit or loss on the mismatch.

Support level   Rate of exchange where central bank intervention occurs either voluntarily (dirty float) or because an upper or lower parity limit has been reached.

Swap The purchase of foreign exchange against another for one value date and the simultaneous sale against another currency for a future value date.

Swap rate Same as Forward Differential, i.e. amount by which spot rate of exchange is adjusted to obtain the forward rate of exchange.

Time deposit An interest-bearing deposit placed for a specific period of time.

Today/tomorrow
Tomorrow/next } Swaps for overnight transactions.

Two-way quotation A quotation for exchange or deposits which includes both a bid and offer price.

Under-valuation Currency is too cheap. The spot rate is below its purchasing power parity.

Value date (1) The settlement date for an exchange contract. (2) The start date for a deposit transaction.

Window-dressing Improving the liquidity of a bank or increasing total or liabilities for a temporary period.

Index

Index

Gul
(